Many blessings ♡ ☺
-libbey Eicher-

STANDING UP TO SCOLIOSIS

*Facing chronic pain and multiple spine surgeries
...with hope*

LIBBEY E. EICHER

CROSSBOOKS
PUBLISHING

CrossBooks™
A Division of LifeWay
1663 Liberty Drive
Bloomington, IN 47403
www.crossbooks.com
Phone: 1-866-879-0502

First published by CrossBooks 7/27/2011

ISBN: 978-1-4627-0572-6 (sc)
ISBN: 978-1-4627-0573-3 (hc)
Library of Congress Control Number: 2011935161

Printed in the United States of America

This book is printed on acid-free paper.

My name is Libbey Eicher. My parents, Sue and Dave Eicher, my sisters, Rebekah and Katie, my grandparents, Virginia and John Bamonte and Grace and Jim Eicher, and many other family members, our church, and a wonderful community of neighbors and friends living in northwest Ohio welcomed me on July 29, 1989 and they, along with my younger sister, Annie and my brother-in-law, Derek (Katie's husband), my teachers at Pettisville High School, co-workers, and my doctors, especially Dr. Munk and Dr. Boachie-Adjei, and caregivers, have been with me on this journey.
I thank each of you for your help and support. You've taught me how to live, and to give. This book is dedicated to you.

Contents

Foreword

If one engages in an activity for a long enough time, one is likely to encounter something that seemingly appears to be quite routine but proves to be anything but typical. Such is this case for me and the medical profession.

When I first met Libbey on 25 July 2005, she had a mild form of what appeared to be quite typical idiopathic, adolescent scoliosis. By virtue of the fact that she was essentially skeletally mature, it was extremely unlikely that the condition would progress and, in fact, I was more concerned with Libbey's accentuated postural thoracic kyphosis as a condition worth addressing with an exercise program. Libbey was an accomplished athlete as a cross country runner and an equestrian so I was confident that she would do the exercises that would help to improve her spinal posture and that she would be able to continue to participate in those activities that she enjoyed so much and was so accomplished in.

What has transpired over the subsequent five and a half years has been anything but straight forward and routine. As if driven by some underlying neurologic abnormality, Libbey's scoliosis did in fact progress quite rapidly and this progression was accompanied by significant spinal decompensation so that Libbey was unable to stand up straight. Initially, in a body cast, Libbey's spinal alignment could be restored quite satisfactorily but this restoration could not be maintained and the scoliosis progressed to the point that surgical intervention seemed to be the only reasonable option.

Because of the extremely unusual progression of Libbey's spinal deformity she needed to be evaluated by a number of other specialists to be certain that there was no obscure, hard to detect, underlying abnormality that might be responsible for Libbey's unusual condition. Prior to Libbey's first operation for her scoliosis, she was seen by three other orthopaedists who specialize in scoliosis surgery, as well as by a pediatric neurologist, pediatric neurosurgeon, and an adolescent psychologist. In addition, she underwent multiple imaging studies in a concerted effort to discover an explanation for her spinal attitude in hopes of avoiding any unnecessary surgery.

When all other reasonable treatment options had been exhausted and surgical intervention seemed to be the only plausible course, Libbey and her family accepted this recommendation with firm resolve and well-founded optimism. However, what seemed to be a very straight-forward solution has proven to be anything but. In spite of the fact that Libbey's initial spinal alignment immediately after the surgery was close to perfect, almost as soon as she stood up the spinal decompensation recurred, and even worsened. In addition, Libbey developed a very unusual problem(s) with her gastro-intestinal system which made it extremely difficult to maintain adequate nutrition so vital to healing.

What subsequently followed were multiple re-evaluations by a multitude of additional specialists and subspecialists including three other orthopaedic spine specialists, three pediatric neurologists, another adolescent psychologist, and two GI specialists. Libbey has endured multiple physical examinations and a myriad of additional imaging studies and additional laboratory tests. She and her family have traveled to Ann Arbor, Michigan, St. Louis, Missouri, Cleveland and Columbus, Ohio, and to New York City in an effort to get to the source of her condition(s) and to achieve a final solution. In addition, after her index spinal operation Libbey has undergone an additional six spinal operations and now, finally, her spinal alignment appears to be acceptable. However, she continues to experience significant lower back discomfort and struggles with being able to eat sufficiently.

That having been said, what is truly amazing about this story is the strength and the fortitude consistently exhibited by Libbey and her family. Throughout this now almost six year ordeal they have been steadfastly focused on the ultimate goal of normalizing Libbey's life and activities. One of Libbey's many goals in life was to become a nurse and to devote her life to medical mission work in the Third World, particularly in Africa. She also wanted to continue to run cross country and to ride horses. She tried very hard to achieve these goals but when she returned to running her back worsened and she recognized that horseback riding would put too much stress on her back so she has put these two activities on the "back burner". When she graduated from high school with a substantial scholarship to attend an out of state college to study nursing she so badly wanted to go but realized that, at that time, she just could not physically endure the challenges of attending school far away from home. Nevertheless she took some college courses locally and now is attending a local college full time with the current goal of becoming a surgical technician. In addition, Libbey did travel to Spain for two weeks with some members of her high school at a time when she was in a great deal of pain, required a back brace to stand up relatively straight and could barely eat even a few bites of food at a time!

Throughout this entire ordeal what has continued to impress me has been the steady resolve exhibited by Libbey and her family. When surgery was proposed they evaluated the options and made informed and considered decisions. On occasion when it was suggested that, since we did not know why Libbey's body was doing what it was, perhaps watching and waiting longer should be considered, Libbey had the sense that everything else had been investigated and tried. She wanted to get on with her life as quickly as possible and reasonable so she elected to proceed with surgery. This was in spite of the fact that Libbey's early post operative periods were consistently miserable for her and for her family-to say the least. I never once heard her bemoan her fate and ask: "Why me?" I have a tremendous amount of respect for Libbey and her family. Libbey and her family have done everything in their power for Libbey to continue to live her life as normally and with as much fulfillment and accomplishment as she possibly could. I know that she will continue to do so and I myself consider it a privilege and an honor to have been able to participate in her care. However, I fully recognize that her success has been and will continue to be very much a tribute to her own personal inner strength, the support of her loving and understanding family and friends and solid, well-grounded and deep Faith.

-Dr. Richard L. Munk, MD

Prologue

I sat on the windowsill looking down at the empty street with tears streaming down my face, wondering if everything I had done was worth it. It was nearly three weeks since I had my sixth major spine surgery, with no real signs of improvement. Were the surgeries worth the suffering and pain I had put myself and my family through? I felt guilty about the money my parents had spent on my medical expenses because the costs were immense, even with the support of friends and family.

Before the first surgery I didn't have pain - mild discomfort, yes, but not pain. My posture was a bit crooked, but it didn't bother me too much. What convinced me to go ahead were the consequences later on if I didn't have the surgery. Now, six surgeries later, the pain was unbearable at times and my posture was awful without my brace on. I stood bent forward and to the right. Rarely would I even allow my parents to see me outside of the brace, because I was so embarrassed. Should I accept this is how I'll look for the rest of my life? I was so tired of test after costly test with no clear answers.

But I'm not a quitter. *God, I know that everything happens for a reason and in your timing, but sometimes I have to wonder how long I'll have to wait for healing.*

At times like these, I remembered the human suffering I had encountered daily in the Dominican Republic a few years earlier.

1 Coincidence? I Think Not!

Excerpt from my spiritual journal. *Jesus, I am Yours. Whatever You have planned for my life, I am ready always. Your plans were uniquely made for me, Father. Use me in Your beautiful ways. Jesus, what you ask of me I will be willing and ready to jump in with both feet. For You don't long for us to jump in with just one foot, You want us fully devoted to You and eager to serve in whatever ways You have paved out for us. Jesus, I am Yours!* *

I was just beginning my freshmen year in high school when my church announced a team mission trip to the Dominican Republic for a week in the spring of 2005. I had been longing to go on a mission trip for many years and so it was agreed that my dad and I would go.

To say it was a life changing experience would be an understatement. As a member of the medical team I filled prescriptions and took the height and weight of the children who came to the clinics. Dad did mechanic work at the guesthouse and helped the construction team prepare a site to build a church. We were so busy we hardly saw each other that week.

It struck me immediately that poverty was a part of daily life in the Dominican Republic – I saw it in the shacks they called home, their tattered clothes, and malnourishment. Yet many seemed so happy and thankful for what little they had. I went home a changed young woman and was bitten by the mission bug.

A few weeks later, just two days after school was out for the summer, I was given a chance to return for four weeks with my friend, Rebekah. Both of us stayed at the guesthouse in San Juan de la Maguana, where Rebekah's grandparents were in charge. This time my assignment varied from week to week depending on what teams came down to help. When medical teams came down, I observed procedures and surgeries performed in the clinic. I saw tumors removed, deformities corrected, and people being able to walk for the first time in years with their new prosthetic limbs. When church teams came down, we helped repaint the classrooms in the school, sang songs with the grade school children, and played volleyball/basketball with the older kids during their lunch break.

I also saw children beg for food at the main gate of the guesthouse and once in awhile a child was given enough food to help feed his/her family for one week. It was puzzling that the same child would be back the next day for more food. Later it was discovered that the child would give the food to the mother, who would then cook for the neighborhood. Everyone would gather whatever small amount they had and share together. This was a very humbling experience for me.

Young children who were financially sponsored went to school and in the first grade were already learning French and English, along with their native Spanish. Rebekah and I went to the school and helped teach the English class for a few days, and we also translated the children's letters into English to send to their sponsored families. I was reminded of all the technology we use in our classrooms here in the United States and how we take these resources for granted.

The smiles of gratefulness from the people just melted my heart. Once again my heart swelled with love for the people, for they had nothing, yet had everything they really needed in life: faith, love, and family.

Coming back home was an adjustment for me. I felt I had way too many "things." I noticed all the food left on plates at restaurants and remembered the children who begged for food. I saw women standing in line to buy piles of clothes at the malls and I remembered the tattered clothes worn day after day. In those first few weeks after coming home I felt guilty about my own life, and angry at the selfishness of my fellow citizens. It took some time for me to balance the lifestyles of both worlds; the rich and poor.

Looking back, I find it no coincidence that God sent me on these mission trips to open my eyes to the important things in life, just months before my own medical problems were to begin.

In the Dominican Republic I had a chance to travel with the medical team where I helped fill prescriptions and take the height and weight of the children. This little girl pictured above sure captured my heart! Looking back, I realize that what I learned and saw those many weeks in the Dominican helped me to get through my many medical trials over the years.

2 The Beginning and Decisions

"Live today fully, expressing gratitude for all you have been, all you are right now, and all you are becoming." Melodie Beattie

It was at the end of the school day in April, 2005 when an announcement came over the loud speakers that if any high school students were interested in volunteering at the local hospital, Fulton County Health Center, we were to meet with the school's guidance counselor. Of course I jumped at the chance, along with my friend Rebekah, because we were both interested in having medical careers. Before I could start volunteering, I had to get a wellness check by my family physician.

It was just to be a simple check to make sure I was "normal." At the appointment, the doctor checked my spine, which was something I had done previously at school. She asked me to bend several times and in different directions. Then she asked me to go out to the waiting room and call my mom back because she wanted to talk with both of us. I thought that was a bit odd, and was a bit apprehensive.

When we came back, the doctor said I had a slight curvature in my spine, called scoliosis, and she wanted me to have an x-ray taken, just as a precaution. She explained that scoliosis is a lateral curvature of the spine and left untreated could cause the curve to worsen over time. My curve was mild, but she wanted me to have an x-ray taken of my spine so that the exact curve could be measured.

A few days later my doctor called mom to explain that the x-ray showed a mild spinal curvature of 16 degrees, but because I was 15 years old and almost finished growing, the chances of the curve worsening was unlikely. Even so, she wanted me to see Dr. Munk, who was a pediatric orthopedic surgeon to be sure she wasn't over-looking something more serious. She left the choice up to us and we decided to have it checked out, just to be sure.

A Mother's Perspective

It seemed like such a 'simple' appointment...who would have guessed it was the beginning of a journey we never expected or wanted to take. Libbey simply had to have a check-up with her family doctor before she would be able to volunteer at the hospital. Libbey had never had a serious health problem and it felt almost like a waste of time to go to the doctor...or so we thought.

Soon after Libbey went back for her 'quick' check-up she was back saying the doctor wanted to talk to me. Those words made my heart skip a beat or two. The doctor asked Libbey to lean forward and showed me the curve in her spine. She said it was a slight curve, not a big problem at all, but one she thought should be checked. So, with the x-ray orders in hand, we went next door to the hospital... where Libbey hoped to volunteer...and soon it was over and we were on our way home with instructions to call the doctor's office the following day for the report.

When I called, I was told she had a 16 degree curvature of the spine- it was considered to be very mild, nothing to worry about. We could either see a specialist or just keep an eye on it ourselves. To be sure, I asked them to set up the appointment for her to be seen and since it was months away, we put the appointment on the calendar and out of our minds. Who would have thought that this "minor" appointment was only the beginning of many appointments, tests, and surgeries to come?

Soon after coming home from the Dominican Republic in July 2005, I saw Dr. Munk, in Toledo, Ohio, for the first time. My spine was now curved at 18 degrees, which is still mild for my age and skeletal maturity (my growth had begun to slow down). Dr. Munk gave me some strengthening exercises to do to help with my posture and told us to come back in four months, just to see if the curve had changed.

Typically, scoliosis occurs in younger, less physically mature teenagers who are just beginning their growth spurt, but my growth plates were just about closed. Also scoliosis is typically hereditary and none of my sisters or parents had it, so I put scoliosis in the back of my mind because I had more important things to think about.

I began running cross country a week later and soon my sophomore year began. My older sister, Katie, was getting married, so we were busy with wedding preparations. I was devoting a lot of time to my beautiful bay colored Arabian horse, Farah. But in early October, my back began to bother me, and it became more painful to run. I was a very good runner and everyone, including me, was surprised that I finished our final seasonal cross country meet so poorly. I wanted to make sure that I was in top shape for the district competition that was only two weeks away. That was when my parents decided I should follow up with Dr. Munk a bit earlier than scheduled to see if my spine had made any changes.

When Dr. Munk examined my spine he said, "That's not the same back I saw just three months ago." The x-rays showed the curve had nearly doubled, to a 34 degree curve. Dr. Munk was rather concerned about the change because it was not typical to progress that quickly in such a short period of time. He scheduled me for an MRI of my brain and entire spine to make sure my vertebrae and spinal cord were normal and advised that I take it easy running until the district cross country meet that was coming up.

I took Dr. Munk's advice and did light running workouts in the days leading up to the district meet. I set a PR (personal record) time for that season, coming in 17th place overall at districts, which secured me a spot in the regional cross country meet!

Later that week the MRI confirmed that my spine was relatively normal, aside from the curve, which was what we wanted to hear. The curve was in the thoracic region, the second of five regions in the spine in this order starting at the top: cervical, thoracic, lumbar, sacral, and coccygeal. Mom, Dad, and I saw Dr. Munk the following week. He explained that he wanted me to be fitted for a back brace to see if that could stop the curve from progressing. I first had to be casted which would be the mold for my brace, and then a few weeks later the brace would be finished.

I just wasn't quite sure about the whole brace idea. It would be quite an adjustment, and I wasn't sure what others at school might think since I didn't know of anyone else in our school that wore a back brace.

During this time, I adopted a horse, One-Across. She was a chestnut colored, retired Standardbred cart racer. When she first came, Farah, my other horse, wasn't sure about sharing her space and it took a while for me to gain One-Across' trust, but carrots and sugar cubes are great incentives, and I had lots of them. Having One-Across complicated my morning walks with

Farah because it was hard to get Farah out of the pasture without One-Across getting loose, which happened more than once!

In November 2005, Dr. Munk casted my upper torso, which was from my hips to my shoulders, for a mold to make me a back brace. I laid on a three inch bar while they casted me. It took a while because they had to wrap individual fiberglass strips around me. When they were done, I had to lie on the table a while longer until my cast dried. It didn't take long, but it got really warm in the cast, which felt good because the room was so cold. They then took an x-ray to check the correction my spine achieved with the cast on. It was not good enough, so the cast was cut off and we did it again. This time it was successful and they told me my back brace would be finished in two weeks.

While waiting for my brace, I wore all of my favorite shirts and jeans because I knew that some of my more fitting clothes wouldn't fit over the brace. I knew it was going to be a big adjustment having to wear a back brace to school every day.

**Excerpt from journal. *Jesus, You knew me when I was in the womb, and You made me special. There are so many portrayals in this world of what a perfect person should do and look like, but Jesus, You made each one of us unique and beautiful in Your sight. It's not what's on the outside that counts, but what's on the inside, which is something I need to remember as I worry about wearing a back brace in public for the first time.* **

At the end of November, I saw the prosthetic/orthotic specialist who made my back brace. When I first saw the brace I panicked because it looked so huge and bulky and I did NOT want to wear it. He then explained he would cut it down, but he needed me to try it on first so he could take some measurements. He made the changes and added Velcro straps to the brace. When I tried the brace on the second time, it hurt my back and was hard to breathe in because it was so tight. But then I decided that if that's what it took to help my spine, I would wear it faithfully, and smile. The specialist was not pleased with how my brace was fitting me even after making changes, so told us to go see what Dr. Munk thought.

Dr. Munk was not pleased with how the brace fit me, but when he told me to take it off he knew immediately why the brace was not fitting well, because my curvature had changed. He sent me for an x-ray which showed that my curve now measured 49 degrees. Dr. Munk was flabbergasted! He had never seen a scoliosis case where the curve had increased so much in such a short period of time. With the cast on, he was able to straighten my spine back down to 11 degrees but without it on, there was quite a difference.

Dr. Munk asked his colleague to examine me for a second opinion of my case. After checking my back they went outside to discuss it. A few minutes later, Dr. Munk came back in and told us that I should still wear the brace even though it didn't fit well. I was to come back in another month and he would see if my spine had made any changes.

After my appointment, mom and I went shopping for some new clothes that would fit over my brace. I thought it was going to be a nightmare but, surprisingly, finding clothes that fit, were stylish, and masked the brace, was not all that difficult - I was just one size bigger.

I was really nervous about going to school for the first time with my brace on because I wasn't sure what people would think. Some of my close friends knew that I was going to have to wear a back brace, but I was still worried. I kept telling myself that people shouldn't look at me any differently because I was still the same person; I just had an added outer shell!

"The Lord does not look at the things man looks at. Man looks at the outward appearance, but the Lord looks at the heart." 1 Samuel 16:7b (NIV) Some people did ask about the back brace but not in a way that made me feel self-conscious.

Going from wearing no brace, to wearing a brace twenty-three hours a day was quite an adjustment. It was really difficult to sleep those first few nights and I just wanted to take the brace off, but I didn't because I wanted the brace to help my spine. I was so sore those first few days. My armpits and hips got rubbed and my muscles ached, but after a few weeks my body got more accustomed to the brace and I was less uncomfortable.

A few days later on December 6, I received a note from the office saying that my mom would pick me up at 11am for a doctor's appointment. My heart sank because I would have to leave in the middle of my science test. Once I was out in the car, mom told me that Dr. Munk decided to put me in another fiberglass cast, only this time for long term, because he thought the cast would stabilize my spine better than the back brace would. I was not too thrilled with this new option because that meant no showers for me for a few weeks.

When we got to the hospital I had to change into a long sock like dress that would lie next to my skin so the cast wouldn't irritate it too much. Then I was wheeled into the casting room and Dr. Munk and others got to work. He lifted me on to the casting bar and tied a strap tightly under my chin to keep my spine as straight as possible. This was really uncomfortable. Wrap by wrap, they plastered my pelvis and hip area and then the rest of my upper torso. When they were done, I had to wait patiently for it to dry and then x-rays were taken. Dr. Munk was pleased that my spine was stabilized down to 16 degrees in the cast.

Over the next few weeks I wasn't able to eat very much with the cast on because my stomach would come out of the belly hole and that put pressure on my back. So every night after I ate, I walked on the treadmill to alleviate my discomfort. But the worst thing about the cast was that I was not able to take showers. Also, I always felt big and bulky with the cast on, and the clothes that fit best were t-shirts and sweat pants, which did not make me feel very pretty. But one night when I was doing my devotions, I came across a verse that helped me to remember what really mattered! *"Your beauty should not come from outward adornment.….Instead, it should be that of your inner self, the unfading beauty of a gentle and quiet spirit, which is of great worth in God's sight." 1 Peter 3:3a-4(NIV)* This verse was a daily reminder to me of where my focus should be, and I had to remember that my cast was going to be on for only a few weeks, not permanently!

Then an exciting and unexpected event happened - I was elected to be the sophomore homecoming attendant! I was really surprised and happy, but anxious too because I was afraid that I would still be in a cast for the homecoming basketball game.

On January 4, 2006, the cast was cut off. Yippee! I had been wearing it for one month and I was really ready for it to come off so I could take a shower.

With the cast off though, my spine curved right back to its abnormal 49 degrees, only I wasn't aware of that at first because I was excited and thought I was straighter. When Dr. Munk walked in my room I knew by the look on his face that I wasn't really standing straighter.

That was when Dr. Munk talked seriously about the possibility of me needing to have the spinal fusion surgery. Before making the final decision, he wanted two other orthopedic surgeons to weigh in with their opinions. He also decided that I should be put into another cast but he assured me it would be off for the homecoming game, which I was grateful for. I was so happy to have the cast off and take a shower again, which is the first thing I did when we got home.

As an attendant I had to go along with the homecoming queen's decision that the attendants were to wear long black dresses. I only had one week until I would be put back in to a cast so mom and I went shopping for a long black dress after school one day. We went to every dress store in the mall and every dress was either too big, or too expensive. Finally at the last store we found the perfect dress that was on sale for only thirty dollars! I was so excited and felt beautiful in my long black dress, and couldn't wait to wear it for homecoming.

The following week, we went to see the other consulting orthopedic surgeon at the University of Toledo Medical Center. He examined me and looked at my x-rays and he agreed with Dr. Munk's opinion that spinal fusion surgery was the only option to correct my curvature. It was nice to have two doctors in agreement.

Then we went directly back to get my new cast made at the Toledo Hospital. Luckily the hospital was close by since we were running late from my previous appointment. When the x-rays showed that my spine was corrected to 9 degrees, Dr. Munk was extremely happy and he assured me that the cast would be off in two weeks - just in time for the homecoming game!

I was really sore for the next few days. After every meal I walked on the treadmill to loosen my cast. I had become very careful about how much I ate each meal because of the discomfort I got in the cast, and I lost weight that I didn't need to lose.

Two weeks later it was time to take off the cast and I could finally breathe deeply. But immediately my spine curved right back to its abnormal curve. I wasn't surprised since the same thing happened the last time my cast was removed, but Dr. Munk seemed disappointed and told us to come back in two weeks to discuss the next step - surgery.

The next day, I went with my parents to Ann Arbor, Michigan for the second consultation. The doctor talked with us about my medical history, checked my reflexes, and had me walk, lie down, and bend for him so he could check my back. Then he looked at all of my x-rays, which was starting to become quite a file. He concluded that surgery would be quite beneficial for me, but he too was puzzled about why my spine had curved so badly and rapidly. So I had three doctors in agreement of a solution. When the consultation was over, we took the opportunity to drive around the beautiful campus of the University of Michigan (even though we were still Buckeye fans at heart!).

Then came our school's local science fair. I entered my project which compared the sugar content and dry matter in stored cucurbita maxima (winter squash). The inspiration for this project came from my observations of malnutrition in the Dominican Republic. A squash plant can produce many large squash, which could then be dried and stored. This could be a cheap and nutritious food source for many in third world countries. My project received high ratings at the local level which allowed me to go on to compete at both the district and state science fair competitions.

Finally, the day of the homecoming game arrived - February 11, 2006. At 11:00, I went to the hairdresser. At 3:00, I put on my makeup, and then came the moment when I could finally put on my pretty black dress that I had been admiring for weeks.

When we arrived at the school, the homecoming court had to pose for newspaper pictures. At 5:40 the ceremony began. As I walked onto the basketball court with the lights shining on us I felt like a princess beside my handsome escort, Alex. For so many weeks I had been in a cast and now I felt free and beautiful in its absence and I stood as straight as I could even though it was uncomfortable. As we walked to our decorated podium and sat down I finally relaxed and enjoyed the game. Afterwards, there was a dance which of course was really fun, even though I can't dance very well but I enjoy doing it! It was my parents' anniversary and they were chaperones since I was a part of the court, so they had a lot of fun too!

* * *

About a week later I saw Dr. Munk again. He found nothing had changed while I was without the cast. He spoke with us about the spinal fusion surgery and penciled it in on May 19 but first he wanted me to see a neurologist, just to be sure he hadn't missed anything neurologically that could have caused my spine to change so quickly. He also put me on iron pills daily to build up my blood supply so I could give blood for the five weeks leading up to my surgery. It was a good appointment and strangely enough, all that talk about surgery didn't make me nervous since I felt comfortable with Dr. Munk and knew I was in good hands.

A week later I saw the neurologist. When we were sitting in the waiting room, I looked at the many other kids in the waiting room with neurological disorders, and I gave thanks that I only had scoliosis to deal with. Scoliosis is a fixable condition where many of the disorders that I saw in the waiting room were permanent.

Nothing appeared neurologically abnormal from his exam of me. He kept commenting on how he liked my smile though, which made me smile even more! He ordered for me to have a blood test and an EMG (electromyography) performed on my muscles, just to make sure there were no underlying neurological problems.

A few days later, I went to our local hospital and got my blood work and EMG done. During the EMG, the doctor poked little needles right below the skin and into the muscles throughout my body. The needles had electrodes on them that were connected to a computer, and so each time he poked me, he could see how well my muscles reacted. Even though it sounds painful it wasn't too bad. In fact, sometimes it tickled. When he was done he told me not to drink anything for thirty minutes because I might spring a leak since I had so many pokes. It took me a while to get his joke! A few days later we found out that both tests came back normal.

On April 15, I donated blood for the first time. Everyone at the Red Cross donation center was very friendly. I was not an easy stick, and it took multiple tries until a vein was found. Luckily I don't mind getting poked too much. After giving blood, I had to sit for 20 minutes while eating snacks (Nutter Butter cookies!), and watching TV. I did this every Wednesday afternoon for five weeks, which meant that I got to miss history class!

A few weeks later there was a blood drive at my school and I found it quite amusing hearing the horror stories that my fellow students had to say about donating blood. Yes the needle was big, but you hardly felt it when donating. I chuckled to myself because donating blood was not bad at all, and I was doing it every week!

In mid April, my parents and I met with Dr. Munk so he could explain the final details of my surgery. We had the last appointment of the day so he didn't have to hurry and we had time to ask questions. My spine was now at a 56 degree curve.

Dr. Munk told us that surgery would last 8 to 12 hours and I would be in the ICU for 3 to 4 days and in the hospital for 6 to 7 days. The incision would cover the entire length of my back and there would be a small incision on my right hip where he would remove some bone marrow and bone graft pieces. Rods would be placed at theT4-L3 region (4th thoracic vertebrae to the 3rd lumbar vertebrae) and the bone grafts would be placed around the rods to help the spinal fusion become solid. I would be put into another fiberglass cast for two weeks after the surgery. When we left, mom asked how I felt about having such a long scar and I told her that I felt it would be my battle scar! That didn't bother me one bit.

At the end of April, I went back to Toledo for a CT scan of my entire spine. This scan was needed so the surgeons could see my spinal cord and could then avoid hitting it when putting in the instrumentation. Hitting the spinal cord is a risk with spinal fusion surgery, and a mistake could result in paralysis.

My May 19 surgery date was stressful for me because school was still in session a week after my surgery which would be final exam week. This meant I had to take my exams early because it was a policy at Pettisville High School that students had to take their final exams even if they had an A in the class. So on May 10th I began to take my final exams for the school year.

A week before surgery I also went in for my pre-op appointment at the Toledo Hospital. I had to be checked over, and have blood work taken. The nurse I had was hoping she'd be taking care of me the morning of my surgery in the pre-op area, and I was also hoping for her too. I was cleared for surgery.

That Sunday was a fun day because it was Mother's Day and all of our grandparents came over for an early supper. Even so, I had to study, and I felt stressed because studying for exams and trying to finish my homework ahead of time, took work and concentration. With surgery looming ahead, I had a lot on my mind, making it difficult to focus.

Throughout my sophomore year, a friend and I had led a Bible study each Monday on purity for freshmen and sophomore girls at our school. We had a good turnout each week and enjoyed the feedback we got from the group. Because I love to bake I took some sort of dessert in each week and everyone seemed to enjoy it! At the end of our last meeting before my surgery they took turns praying for me. It touched me that they would care so much.

That night I took a last ride on my beautiful horse, Farah. She could be a little ornery sometimes when she was in a bad mood but that night she behaved like an angel. I understood why the doctors had encouraged me not to ride following my surgery but it was hard to let that go, and made that last ride all the more meaningful.

I made it through the rest of that week somehow, completing all of my projects and exams; however I did miss out on dissecting frogs in biology which was disappointing for me.

The day before my surgery I stayed home from school. I had to do some pre-surgical prep and then I had some chores to do around the house and barn such as cleaning my room, and Farah's water trough. (She really appreciated that.) The day went so fast! I spent most of the afternoon with Farah, brushing her and telling her everything. It was so peaceful sitting on the fence listening to Farah swish the flies away with her tail while watching the sunset, talking to Jesus, and anticipating what the next day would bring.

Throughout that day my mom had taken pictures of my back so we could compare them with my post-op pictures. She also marked my height against our kitchen door to see if I would "grow" an inch or two after the surgery, since we were told that could happen.

That evening my parents took Annie to Katie and Derek's house so she wouldn't have to wake up with us so early. They would come to the hospital, but a little later than we would.

It wasn't until I went to bed that I realized I was a little bit nervous, but not nearly as much as I thought I'd be. I think it helped that I had seen surgeries in the Dominican Republic and even wanted to be a surgical nurse someday. I knew I was tough and had a high pain tolerance so I thought I'd be back up and ready to go soon after surgery.

When sleep was difficult that night I prayed for Dr. Munk and his colleague because I knew they'd have a long and tiring day ahead of them. When flipping through my bible I came across a few verses in Psalms that gave me comfort for my racing heart. *"He will cover you with his feathers, and under his wings you will find refuge…For he will command his angels concerning you to guard you in all your ways; they will lift you up in their hands." Psalm 91:4a, 11-12a (NIV)* No matter what the outcome of the surgery, I knew that God's protection would be over me and the doctors and nurses involved. Healing is always possible through God, but my family and I also believe that God works through the surgeon to give him/her the ability and talent to help in the healing process of their patient. I was well aware of the risks involved in my surgery, but I still wasn't really aware of the magnitude of it all.

**Excerpt from journal. *Jesus, life is full of many mountains and valleys. Life can be hard and many times the way to the top of the mountain looks endless, but Jesus, I know You have the power to move those mountains. It may not be in the way we had thought, but You lift us up when times get hard and help us through to the other side. I love You Jesus so much and thank You for conquering the grave and giving us hope again!* **

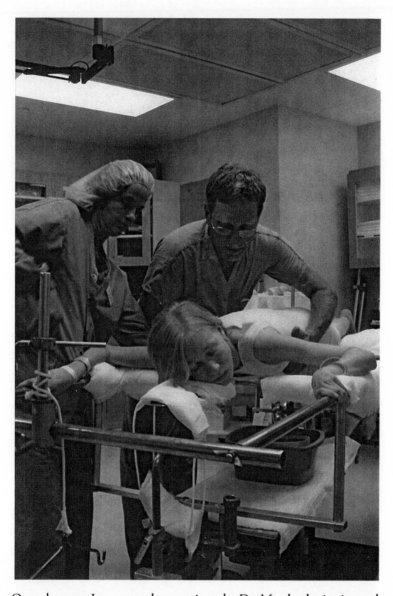

Over the years I was casted many times by Dr. Munk who is pictured. Sometimes it was to make a mold for a back brace where the cast was cut off of me after it had dried, while other times I had to keep the cast on for a few weeks.

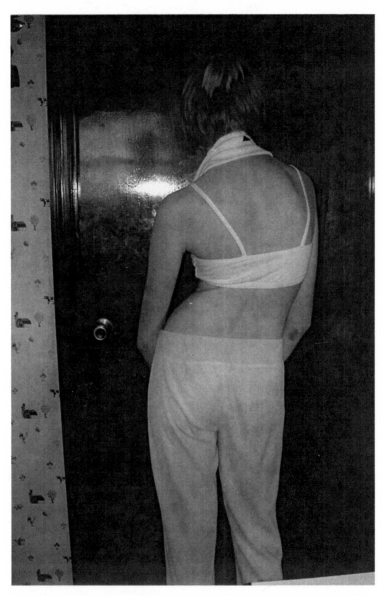

This picture was taken May 18, 2006, which was the day before my first spinal fusion surgery. My curve was 56 degrees.

3 Surgery #1

"God helps the sick in two ways, through the science of medicine and through the science of faith and prayer." Norman Vincent Peale

On the morning of May 19, 2006, I woke up at 3:45 a.m. and did 150 sit-ups because I wasn't sure if I would have the flexibility to do them after surgery. Before we left for the hospital, my parents came to my room and then gave me a hug, and then we held hands and prayed because we knew once we got to the hospital we would get caught up in the pre-op busyness.

We took both cars so mom and dad would be able to go back and forth while I was in the hospital. As soon as we left, it started pouring down rain. The rain was coming down so hard that it was difficult to see anything and it was pitch black outside. I was driving with dad and I kept mom's taillights in view. Driving in such conditions did me good because it kept my mind focused on the road ahead instead of my upcoming surgery.

And then without thinking I popped in a favorite CD of mine and suddenly the artist was singing about God's healing rain. Driving to the hospital, I felt as if my healing rain was falling down. As the rain was pounding down on the windshield, I felt that it was God's reminder to me that he had everything under control no matter what the outcome would be that day.

Nearly an hour later, we were at the Toledo Hospital and had no trouble parking both cars right next to each other. I carried my back brace and dad brought my book bag with all of my things in it. We were early so we sat down in the waiting room and relaxed. Ha, who can relax before surgery? The butterflies in my stomach were now wide awake. A few minutes later a very nice man came for all of us who were scheduled for surgery. I was given a corner room where I had a bit more privacy. I changed into a huge blue gown and put my footies on. Then my nurse, who I had had a week earlier, came and checked my blood pressure, pulse, oxygen level, and attempted to start an IV line. I was never an easy stick. The anesthesiologist then introduced himself, asked some questions about my medical history, and then Dr. Munk and his colleague, who was assisting, came in, dressed in their scrubs. They were ready!

When they left, the nurse let my whole family come in to wish me well, as long as we kept the tone down. The room was very crowded, but full of love! It meant so much to me to have my parents and sisters all there. I know we were all nervous and a little anxious but we were all talking and trying to make each other laugh. And then our pastor, Brad, came down to pray with us. With my eyes closed, I sensed the Holy Spirit moving throughout my room. I knew that so many people were lifting both my family and me, and all the medical personnel involved in my care, up in prayer which gave me comfort. We were all in this together.

My friends from high school, Rachel and Rebekah, came in for a quick visit. They had driven all the way to Toledo before school started just to see me. This was totally unexpected. What great friends! They brought with them a card everyone in our class had signed, and a video of our classmates wishing me good luck and singing silly songs to cheer me up. They had been busy for weeks while I was absent at doctor's appointments or giving blood. It was so encouraging to know how much everyone cared about me!

Then my OR nurses came in and said it was time to go and everyone was in a hurry. They, along with Helen, Dr. Munk's nurse, wheeled me out and down a hallway until we reached a corner called the "kiss corner" because that's where I had to tell everyone goodbye and reassure them not to worry. Then they wheeled me through the big double doors and down many hallways until we reached my operating room. The lights were really dimmed and there were many machines set up. The surgical table had many black pads on it.

Everyone was ready to get started and was waiting for me to go to sleep. Helen held my hand and kept making me smile while the anesthesiologist hooked cold leads on my chest to monitor my heart. Then he held an oxygen mask above my mouth and nose and told me to breathe deeply. That's all I remember. It was 7:30 am, right on schedule.

A Sister's (Rebekah) Perspective

When I first heard that Libbey had scoliosis I wasn't sure what it was exactly. I had a general idea, but I didn't realize how extreme the surgery had to be to correct it. It seemed that with the one surgery it should be corrected and, once she had healed, things would go back to normal. The day of the surgery was an early day, and I rode down to the hospital with Katie, Derek, and Annie. It was a pretty quiet ride because we were tired, but most of all nervous. I remember praying most of the way down for a fast and successful surgery. We saw Libbey and she was in good spirits. We were all talking and just enjoying being together. When they came to take her back, it just kind of made your heart jump into your throat. She went around the kissing corner and we went out to the waiting room….to do just that….wait. This surgery was very long, but when her doctor came out he seemed pretty positive with how things had gone. That was a relief! She always seemed to have a hard time with the post-op part of things, so that was a bumpy ride waiting to find out what exactly was going on.

Nine hours later, around 4:30 that afternoon, Dr. Munk, went out into the waiting room and told my family that all had gone well. He then showed them some x-rays that had been taken during surgery. They showed a straight spine with a lot of hardware and screws. My family waited two more hours until they could see me in the pediatric ICU. Dr. Munk warned them that my face would be puffy because I had laid face down for many hours. My dad told me later that my face was so puffy that I really didn't even look like myself.

A Sister's (Annie) Perspective

At the time of Libbey's first surgery, I was a sixth grader at Pettisville Elementary School. I had never heard of scoliosis before Libbey was diagnosed, so when I found out she was having surgery, I didn't know what to expect. After waiting for nine hours, I was just expecting her to come out of surgery and two days later be fine, just like she was before surgery. So imagine my surprise when I walked in and saw her in the Pediatric Intensive Care Unit for the first time, seeing her attached to all the tubes and monitors. That is not what I was expecting her to look like afterwards. After the initial shock wore off, it was extremely difficult for me to go and see her in the ICU, because seeing her like that upset me and made me cry.

My first memories were of unbearable pain later that evening. I think I drifted off again under more pain and sleep medication, which was such a relief at this point. I woke up with a central line in my neck and an IV in both hands. There was a nasogastric (NG) tube down my nose and into my stomach to drain out the anesthetic, an oxygen line in my nose, and a urinary catheter. My mom told me later that I kept setting off the alarms that night because my pulse was so low and nurses were in and out all night. I didn't really wake up again until noon on Saturday, but then I was in a lot of pain, and after more much needed pain medication, I slept again.

A Sister's (Katie) Perspective

After you were taken to the pediatric intensive care unit after the very first surgery, the nurse was attempting to take a blood sample from you. Unfortunately for me, she did not get her syringe in your IV fast enough and blood came squirting out of your IV! It was so gross and I almost had to step outside your room! I do not handle seeing blood very well!

On Sunday morning my left lung collapsed. So I began breathing treatments every four hours, day and night. This was not fun. During one of my afternoon respiratory treatments they made me sit up, which was so painful. In fact, I was in so much pain and was so groggy from all the pain medication that I couldn't support myself when sitting up. My nurse put a pillow behind my back and tried to hold me up. When the nurse tired, my dad held me up. Then dad got tired too and then Derek took over. Then they let me lie down again after the treatment was over. I have a high pain tolerance and so going into this surgery, I thought it would be no big deal, but was I wrong.

I was always so hot so the nurses set a huge box fan right next to the head of my bed. That felt good to me but mom and dad were freezing since my room was already very cool from the air conditioning. My temperature kept slowly rising, even with medication, and reached 103.1 degrees. The nurses said that they would need to do something to bring it down if it went any higher, but thankfully it never did.

Early every morning two radiology techs came in and took chest x-rays, which I was not thrilled about. They moved the bed and placed me almost in a sitting position, which was pure torture for me. They were so nice about it, but I was in so much pain.

Soon a third of my right lung collapsed also so I was given more intense respiratory treatments to try to inflate my lung without going back on the ventilator, which is what the ICU doctor told me they'd have to do if my lungs didn't inflate on their own. I really did not want that to happen.

Tuesday was a rough one. My stomach was so bloated from the anesthetic that the stomach aches made my back hurt. (Is that possible?) When my drainage tube was taken out of my nose my throat felt so much better, and that was a positive for the day.

That night the pain came back with a vengeance, and I hardly slept. Every two hours the nurses would come in my room and roll me on to my side, just to keep me moving. I had two nurses that night in ICU and they tried to keep me comfortable, but I was so hot and in agony and nothing seemed to help. Finally I fell asleep from pure exhaustion in the early morning hours.

Suddenly I was awake again in a panic because the nurses were standing over me trying to reinsert a drainage tube into my nose to help drain out some of the acid in my stomach. I grabbed the one nurse's arm in confusion, and they spoke reassuringly to me until I was finally aware of what they were doing and where I was. It was a long night.

Dr. Munk came in the next morning, rolled me over, and changed the dressing that was on my back. He tried to make me comfortable by moving me around until I found a comfortable way to lie. He even filled up bags of ice to put along my back to try to numb the pain. This helped immensely.

When he left, my nurses helped me in to a chair and served me a liquid diet tray. I couldn't eat a thing and had absolutely no appetite. I had already gone more than five days without eating, so they gave me two more IV fluids, one containing lipids and the other consisting of nutrients that my body needed called TPN. They looked just like bags of mountain dew and milk.

I watched the finale of American Idol that evening through half closed eyes and just when I was getting very sleepy, the nurses came to get me up for my first walk. Oh, was it painful. My mom was still there and she said it looked as if I had suffered a stroke. I dragged one foot and my head hung to the right side. I really could not go very far and was absolutely exhausted by the time I was helped back in to bed.

The next morning, Thursday, they finally washed my hair along with the usual wipe off "bath" called the "fluff n buff". Often they would pamper me with some of their own fancy creams, which made both my room and me smell wonderful and it was appreciated!

That afternoon I was taken to have a new cast made. My nurse from the ICU came to the casting room to give me pain medication before they did anything. This was so thoughtful of her because it was painful lying on that three inch bar. Just before Dr. Munk finished, I apparently passed out. My mom told me later that he finished very quickly, and I was taken back to the pediatric ICU and hooked up to the monitors just to be on the safe side because they weren't sure what had happened. When I came to, Dr. Munk returned and helped me in to a chair so he could trim my cast to fit me.

That evening I was moved to the regular pediatric floor, which was very busy and loud compared to the ICU. To pass time, mom and I took short walks in the hallway and watched the movie, Titanic, because it's a long movie and we had the time!

Rebekah and Rachel, my two very special friends from school, came to visit me that evening but it wasn't a good visit because I was in so much pain. I tried to hold in the pain, but this pain was far worse than any I'd ever experienced. That night after they left, it was just mom and me sitting on the bed. I finally broke down and cried telling mom to just shoot me, but she didn't think that was a good idea. I just didn't think I could go on with so much pain much longer.

A Mother's Perspective

I will never forget one of Libbey's "darkest" nights following her first surgery. We thought we were prepared for surgery. We knew there would be pain, but no one told us how awful the pain was going to be. We were totally unprepared for it and felt completely helpless in helping Libbey through the pain - a relentless and unbearable pain. Would it ever stop, would it ever get easier for her, could the nurses find just the right combination of drugs to make her comfortable....even for just a few minutes?

I am the mom, I had been making her feel "all better" for years with a Snoopy band-aid, a hug, or making her laugh. All of a sudden, there was absolutely nothing I could do for her to ease the pain, make it "'go away," find a comfort zone. I spent those nights with her, sitting in a chair by the bed, just in case she needed or wanted me. I couldn't imagine leaving her with that pain, alone in that dark room.

She seemed to like to listen to worship CD's during the nights as she fought through the pain. Tonight was no different - it was "bedtime" - so I popped in a CD. Then I covered her up and went back to my chair and covered up. It was peaceful with the music playing. Then, about 2am, I heard Libbey, but I couldn't understand what she was saying. So I jumped out of my chair and went to her side and then I heard her loud and clear, and the words she spoke took my breath away....all she said was, "I can't do this anymore." What do I do - what should I say? Here I stand, trying to find words to comfort her, but all I want to do is cry. But I can't. I am the mom. I have to be strong, for her, but I've never felt so weak and helpless. I can't remember exactly what I said that night. Maybe I've blocked it out of my mind, I just don't know. All I remember thinking was, I'm Libbey's mom and I can't do anything for her....what kind of mom am I anyway?

On Saturday, Dr. Munk's nurse, Helen, called me to ask what I'd like to eat. I really needed to eat something, and she was willing to go get me anything, but all I could think of was a smoothie. She was going to see what she could do! A little awhile later, Helen came in carrying two strawberry smoothies, one for me and one for mom. I couldn't drink very much because it gave me a stomach ache, but it was delicious and hit the spot!

Later, my older sister, Rebekah and mom took me outside in a wheelchair and around the park. It was great to get some fresh air and feel the sun on my face, although it was so hot out, especially with my cast on. Going outside was just what I needed to raise my spirits up. That afternoon, I was given some much needed pain medication that put me to sleep. I understand that one of my good friends and her sister came to visit me, but I slept through their entire visit, even while they ate pizza in my room with my parents. That was how out of it I was, I never even noticed!

Sunday afternoon, ten days after surgery, Dr. Munk came in with a big smile on his face and said that I could leave that afternoon or the next morning. I voted for an immediate departure, since that would save money, even though I knew it would be hot at home without air conditioning. When dad came to pick mom and me up later that afternoon, the drive home seemed to take forever- I felt every little bump in the road - but it sure felt fine to be home again and in my own bed. Before surgery, for years, I didn't have a bed in my room because I thought it took up too much space. Instead, I slept in a sleeping bag on my floor. Seeing how difficult it was for me to move around in the hospital, mom and dad decided that my bed needed to be set up again because there would be no way I'd be able to get down and up from the floor.

23

Just two days after coming home, I fell out of bed one afternoon while taking a nap because I was so used to sleeping on the floor, not a bed!

Over the next few days I was amazed at the amount of support that so many people gave to my family and me. Each day I received several cards in the mail, which was just the kind of encouragement I needed since I was not feeling great at all. I may have been out of the hospital, but it was so nice to know that people were still praying for my healing. Also, our church had lined up people to bring us meals for two weeks after I came home. Often times I really couldn't eat what people brought but I was so grateful to the generosity of the many who provided for us. Lasagna was the dish of choice for many to bring, so it was fun to see all the different ways lasagna could be made.

**Excerpt from journal. *Jesus, there are so many road blocks throughout our lives, but You have a purpose for all of them. I will run the race of life, Jesus, for I know that You are near me, and are always there to embrace me when I am faced with difficulties. I am so grateful for Your everlasting love for me Father.* **

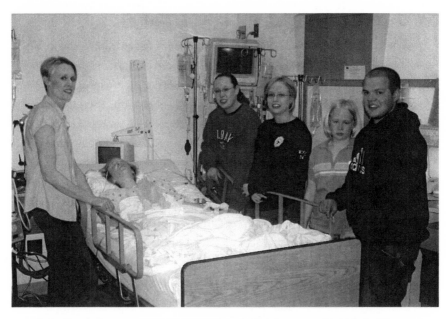

My cheering section which included (left) Mom, me, Rebekah, Katie, Annie, and my brother in law, Derek, while Dad was taking the picture. This was taken just a few hours after my first surgery on May 19, 2006 in the Pediatric Intensive Care Unit. Luckily I was on heavy pain killers so I could escape the pain for a little while.

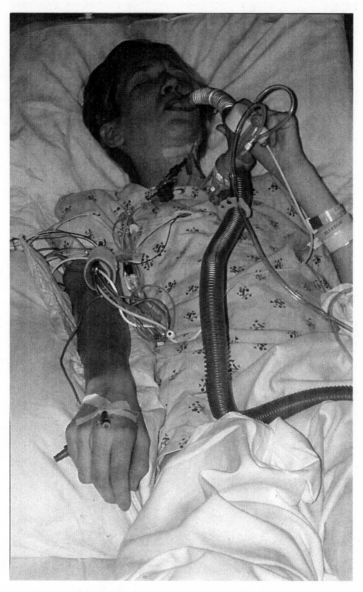

Every few hours I had to have intense breathing treatments to try to get my left lung to inflate again after it collapsed.

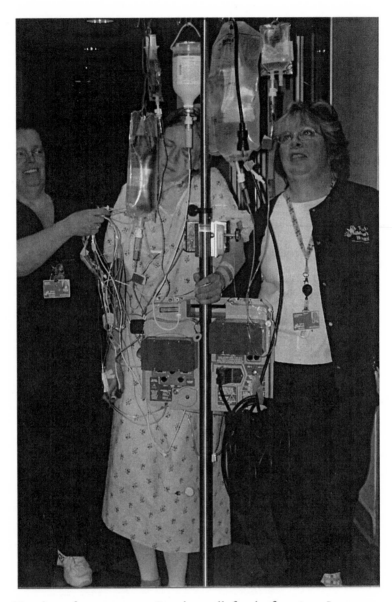

Five days after my surgery I took a walk for the first time. It was very painful and I felt as if my back was going to split open, but with the support of my nurses, I was able to walk several feet.

4 Taking it One Day at a Time

"We must leave it to God to answer our prayers in His own wisest way. Sometimes, we are so impatient and think that God does not answer. God always answers! He never fails! Be still. Abide in Him."
Mrs. Charles E. Cowman

My days consisted of waking up around 10 o'clock, attempting to eat lunch around 11, taking a sponge bath around noon, and then couch time with crossword puzzles. Mom could usually persuade me to take a walk because I needed to get up and about. Then I napped all afternoon. I'd attempt to eat supper around 6:00 and then off to bed by 11:30. But I dreaded the night because the pain was always worse.

A few nights after I had gotten home from the hospital, many of my teammates from the track team came over to visit, after the end of the year track potluck. It was so nice having visitors, and had a way of cheering me up! They brought two plates full of food from the potluck which was so thoughtful of them, although I had so many problems eating anything.

My cast was really loose because my stomach was no longer bloated from the anesthetic, and I wasn't able to eat much of anything because my stomach hurt every time I ate, so I lost weight. On those really hot days I could feel the sweat running down my back, which was gross and made me all the more itchy under my cast. I often would have mom or dad use a ruler to scratch my back under the cast which did help some!

My mom's a wonderful cook and she kept making my favorite foods but nothing could coax me to eat. One day I told her a strawberry rhubarb pie might taste a little good. My mom is a hostess at a restaurant where they make the best strawberry rhubarb pies, so she jumped at the chance to get some food in me. She called her restaurant, pulled a few strings, and that afternoon, she picked up a fresh, hot strawberry rhubarb pie. I couldn't eat much, but what little I did have of that pie tasted like heaven.

On June 7, 2006, nearly two weeks after surgery, mom and I went to see Dr. Munk for my post op appointment. It was the first time I had left home in more than a week so it was great to get out of the house and see something other than cornfields!

Helen cut my cast off and I felt so light without it, but very itchy as well. Dr Munk took the extra bandage off my back and checked my incision, which was healing very well, but when I stood up I was bent forward, which was puzzling to him. Dr. Munk took me out into the hallway and showed me how to do some exercises to help strengthen the muscles in my back. There was a whole crowd of people watching me as I tried to walk up and down the hallway, including, Dr. Munk and his colleague, their nurses and a resident medical student who was shadowing Dr. Munk at the time. I felt very self-conscious especially because I was afraid I'd fall since I was so wobbly on my feet. I looked awful and they looked at mom like, "what on earth have we done to her?" I would've rather gotten the attention from everyone some other way.

Then they weighed me. That had now become another problem because I was down to 96 pounds on my 5 feet 5 inch frame, which was nine pounds less than my pre-op weight. I was told to work on my exercises throughout the day every day, and to come back in two weeks to see if there were changes.

I enjoyed sitting in the lawn chairs on our porch, feeling the summer breeze on my face, hearing the birds chirping, and listening to the bugs buzzing. *"Look at the birds of the air; they do not sow or reap or store away in barns, and yet your heavenly Father feeds them. Are you not much more valuable than they? Who of you by worrying can add a single hour to his life?" Matthew 6:26-27 (NIV)* Seeing birds flying about reminded me of this verse and that God cares about every little thing whether big or small. He was taking care of me, so I needed to trust that things would work out in his timing, although at times, it was difficult.

The following week I saw our family physician, about my lack of appetite. Because of the pain I was experiencing every time I ate, she scheduled an ultrasound of my liver, gallbladder, and spleen for the next morning.

Well, everything was not all right. My gallbladder was full of sludge. My doctor was notified and she had me admitted to the Fulton County Health Center, thinking my gallbladder needed to be removed. I was put on IV fluids for dehydration and that night I was told by the general surgeon that it seemed, with proper hydration, the sludge would move out of my gallbladder in time, so that was good news. Four long days later I was finally back home.

The following Wednesday, I saw Dr. Munk again. I had lost another pound and was still hunched forward and in a lot of pain, even though I did my strengthening exercises faithfully every day. He was very concerned and decided for me to have an upper GI/ barium swallow test done the following day to see if my stomach was tethered, which might be pulling me forward so much. For the test, a few days later, I had to drink two glasses of a thick barium solution, and then a series of x-rays were taken to follow the barium through my digestive tract. That test showed nothing abnormal, so we still didn't know why I was leaning forward and unable to eat.

That night, mom called Helen and cried because she just didn't know what to do with me. She knew that something was wrong because I was still hunched over, had lots of lower back pain, and still couldn't eat much. I did my exercises daily, even though they really hurt. Helen called mom the next day and made me another appointment with Dr. Munk the following week. I couldn't wait for that appointment because something was just not right and I was tired of feeling miserable and utterly exhausted.

At that appointment, Dr. Munk examined me very closely. He took more x-rays, and from a side view, my spine was straight up and down from my neck to my pelvis, which is also known as flat back syndrome. (Normally the spine is supposed to have a slight curve in the lumbar and thoracic regions of the spine to help with balance, and create less stress on your lower vertebrae.) He scheduled a CT scan to make sure that the screws and rods were in right and had not loosened or shifted. The scan showed that the hardware was fine and in the correct places.

As Dr. Munk, mom, and I were walking slowly down the hallway after I had had my CT scan, Dr. Munk told us he was going to schedule surgery for me on July 14, which was a little over two weeks away. He wanted to reposition my rods and make a more natural curve in my lumbar spine so that I wouldn't be so hunched over and could possibly alleviate some pain. On the way home, mom and I felt somewhat relieved because something needed to be done; I couldn't stand how much pain I was in, and I was always exhausted. Walking was very painful, and eating was nonexistent.

The days just could not go fast enough -I was actually looking forward to this surgery. Even though I dreaded the pain this surgery would bring, I knew it would be worth it if it relieved the chronic pain I was dealing with.

My friends, Rebekah and Rachel were spending the month of July in the Dominican Republic. As disappointed as I was that I was not able to go with them, I was grateful I had the opportunity to go the summer before. We emailed back and forth daily and, although I wasn't physically with them, I could laugh and picture the people and places they wrote about. Those daily emails certainly lifted my spirits, and I looked forward to them!

On Monday, July 10, I had my pre op appointment at Toledo Hospital and I was cleared for another surgery. Then we stopped by for a pre-op appointment with Dr. Munk. He had just returned from a medical conference where he presented my case to get other surgeons' input. He was hoping that I would be magically straight when he came back home, but that just didn't happen yet. He told me that he even sent me a post card!

My surgery was to last about 4 hours and I would need to stay in the hospital through the weekend because my surgery was on a Friday. Dr. Munk and his colleague were going to bend my rods in the lumbar area and loosen some of the screws. I was ready!

"Look to the Lord and his strength; seek his face always. Remember the wonders he has done." Psalm 105:4-5a (NIV)

5 Surgery #2

"For you created my inmost being; you knit me together in my mother's womb. I praise you because I am fearfully and wonderfully made; your works are wonderful, I know that full well." Psalm 139:13-14 (NIV)

The night before my surgery I found myself reading through Ephesians, which to me is a book of encouragement and hope, as I anticipated another surgery the next morning. Ephesians 3:17-20 (NIV) states: *"And I pray that you, being rooted and established in love, may have power, together with all the saints to grasp how wide and long and high and deep is the love of Christ, and to know this love that surpasses knowledge—that you may be filled to the measure of all the fullness of God. Now to him who is able to do immeasurably more than all we ask or imagine, according to his power that is at work within us."* There is no way for any of us to be able to fully measure God's love because it is infinite. God's love for us has no ending and goes on forever and ever. It is so profound to know that someone can love me that much! God always hears our prayers and desires, but He doesn't always give us exactly what we ask of Him because He is able to do *"immeasurably more than all we ask or imagine."* God's plans are far better than my own. I felt overcome with peace as I anticipated surgery in just a few hours, because I knew God already had the outcome planned and I needed to trust that whatever that was, He had a purpose for it.

July 14, 2006 finally came. We arrived at the Toledo Hospital just in time and again they whisked me off in to the pre-op area. Soon after I was all prepped and ready to go, Annie, Katie, and Derek came in and trailing behind them was Rebekah and Helen. The curtain was closed and we were told to be quiet. Now that's a tall order for my family because when we get together, we can get loud. It didn't help that I was in the first room so everyone walking in the pre-op area could hear us if we were too loud! So we were reminded several times to quiet down, but the staff was understanding and many times joked along with us! My doctors stopped by and suddenly we had nine people in my tiny room. Right before it was time for me to leave, our pastor arrived and we all held hands in a circle and prayed. I could really feel God's peace come over me and once again I was reminded that He had everything under control.

As I was wheeled away around 1pm, my family trailed behind me to the kiss corner where everyone said their goodbyes and I gave them a kiss. I was wheeled through the "personnel only" doors and down many hallways until we reached my OR. Those huge surgical lights greeted me as the big double doors opened and there were many machines and staff standing by. The nurses kept making me laugh which made me relax. Helen and Kitty, who was also a nurse at the office, and observing my surgery that day, were also right by my bedside. The anesthesiologist hooked me up to the cardiac monitor and then put the oxygen mask above my nose and mouth and I soon drifted off to sleep.

The surgery went well and I was wheeled into recovery a little past five. I was slow to come out of the anesthetic and I had trouble breathing. My respirations would go up really high, and then the next minute they would be dropping down really low. A Non-Rebreather Oxygen Mask was put on me to assist in my breathing, but that still didn't help much so they put a tube down the other side of my nose to suction out my esophagus. This actually helped, once they took the tube out.

My parents were finally allowed to see me around 10 p.m., and soon after I was taken to the pediatric ICU. I was very nauseous and I vomited twice. Not a great way to greet my nurses. It felt as if my incision was being torn open. I don't remember much more that night because I was exhausted and went right to sleep after receiving some pain medication.

I slept through most of Saturday and finally on Sunday afternoon the ICU nurse helped me sit up. At first it was very painful but after repeatedly sitting up that day the pain lessened.

Each night it was comforting to lie in bed and listen to a worship CD as I fell asleep. Generally I'd be asleep before I was halfway through a CD but I remember one song in particular at the beginning sung by Adrienne Liesching and Geoff Moore that meant a lot to me. *"In Christ alone my hope is found, He is my light, my strength, my song. This cornerstone this solid ground, firm through the fiercest drought and storm. What heights of love, what depths of peace, when fears are stilled, when strivings cease. My Comforter, my All in All; Here in the love of Christ I stand."* The post-op pain was horrible, but in Christ alone, my hope for healing was found. I knew He had a reason for me enduring the pain, although at times, the pain seemed more than I could bear.

On Monday morning I got up and tried to take a longer walk. I was a little wobbly. Later Dr. Munk watched me walk down the hallway. I wasn't hunched forward anymore but now I was leaning slightly to my right side. That night I was taken to the regular pediatric floor and was delighted to find in the morning that I had a great window view from my bed.

Later on Tuesday, Dr. Munk made a new cast for me. This time, instead of lying on my back, I had to lie with my stomach on that 3 inch bar while he lifted my legs up with pillows to make my spine arch while he casted me. It didn't take too long, but I was glad when it was over. Afterwards I was sore and it hurt to take deep breaths but I was able to take short walks which helped. Later on that evening, Dad and Annie brought supper so that when my dinner tray came we could all "eat" together. I'm sure my "eating" consisted more of pushing my food around my plate and taking teeny bites. I wanted Dad to eat some of my food so that way it looked as if I ate something when my nurse came back to check, but he wasn't agreeing to my plan!

When I walked, my right leg always acted weaker than my left leg. So I had another EMG to test the muscles in my legs and around my spine. It confirmed that my right leg was slightly weaker than my left leg, but we already assumed that.

The next evening, Dr. Munk walked into my room with a big smile on his face and said those magic words, I could go home! I was discharged with instructions to do my leg strengthening exercises on a regular basis. Again, the ride home seemed so long and bumpy but I was so happy to be home again. I went right to sleep soon after and slept through till late the next morning. Finally an uninterrupted night of sleep!

Dr. Munk's post card from Aruba was waiting for me when I got home. How cool was that?!

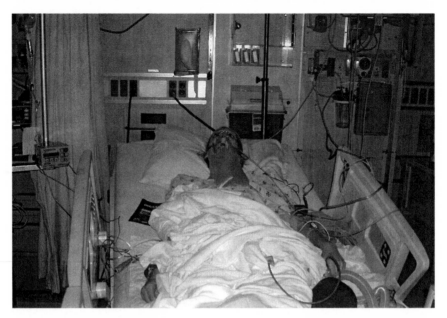

Surgery number two was on July 14, 2006. The surgery was four hours long, but because of my condition I was in recovery longer than I was in surgery, five hours.

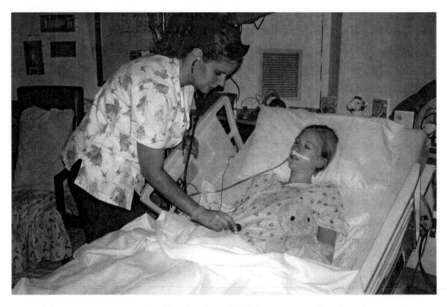

After my surgeries, I often had an NG (nasogastric) tube that went down my nose and into my stomach to help with the postoperative nausea and bloating and to suction out the contents in my stomach.

6 My New Type of Therapy...a Dog!

"Whom have I in heaven but you? And earth has nothing I desire besides you. My flesh and my heart may fail, but God is the strength of my heart and my portion forever. Psalm 73: 25-26 (NIV)

The next night the whole family came over to our house as a surprise. For several weeks my parents had been asking me what I wanted for my birthday, as if they were really excited about something. I kept telling them I didn't need anything, especially since I knew there would be plenty of medical bills to pay.

I was told to sit in a chair on the deck and close my eyes while dad went around front to get something. All of a sudden something furry and squirmy was plopped on my lap, and when I opened my eyes, there was the cutest black labradoodle puppy I could imagine. I named him Lenney.

He was my therapy dog because I took him out for short walks throughout the day to help me gain strength back and to get me out and exercising. It was fun to have a dog around the house again, and he lifted my spirits. I couldn't pet him as much as I wanted to though because my cast prevented me from bending.

A Dog's (Lenney) Perspective

It's a "dog's life," for sure. Usually that means someone's living a life of ease but I'm here to tell you that my life's a busy one.

My birth mom's name is Libby and my adoptive mom's name is also Libbey....I think I was meant to live here! I came to live at Libbey's house right after her second surgery, when she was having a miserable summer. She was in pain, couldn't eat, and was just tired of feeling....well, miserable. Her birthday was coming up and her parents knew she needed an awesome gift. (That's me.) Libbey's mom kept saying, "I just keep coming up with getting her a dog...she would love it." So, to make a long story short, they found me two weeks before the 2nd surgery, but kept me at my birth home until Libbey came home from the hospital. Imagine her surprise when I was placed in her lap...she was thrilled!

Since then I've made her smile when she didn't feel like smiling, got her outside to walk and exercise when she didn't really want to, and I even threw up in her room during the night a few times so she's had to take me outside in the middle of the night too....she was thrilled with that! Actually through all of this I've helped the entire family with my wet nose and wagging tail. I listen, I snuggle, and when anyone's "down" somehow I manage to cheer them up. I often hear them say they don't know how they went so long without me and I make the family complete. I even have them trained a bit. At first, I wasn't allowed on the couch, but now that they see how comfortable I am, they don't bother me anymore. I even sneak on to Libbey's bed when she's not looking, but don't tell her. So if this is a 'dogs life," I'm all for it!

I followed up with Dr. Munk a week later. It was hot and humid at the end of July. I was baking in my cast. That afternoon they cut the cast off and boy did that feel good, but was I ever itchy!

Dr. Munk popped in on his way to see another patient to give me a birthday present - a book all about labradoodles and how to care for them and a vet book by James Herriot! Those books were so thoughtful and would keep me busy for awhile! We had just posted a birthday card to him (his birthday was just three days before mine) with a Snoopy tie, to add to his diverse collection of cute decorative ties. I was his last patient of the day so while we waited we chatted with the staff in his office who now knew us very well. When he finally opened the door, guess what? He was wearing the Snoopy tie we had just gotten him, and looked very stylish with it on!

Without my cast I still leaned slightly to the right. I had also lost another pound or two, bringing me in at a grand total of 92.5 lbs. I was surprised by that because by then I had started eating more, but probably not much with enough calories because it was mostly fresh fruit and vegetables from the garden. We were also surprised that my weaker right leg was actually bigger than my stronger left leg.

Dr. Munk put my cast back on and wrapped ace bandages around it to keep it from falling off. He said I would be getting a new back brace to give my back more support, and that I'd need to wear it for four months. Being his last patient of the day, I got a little extra time with Dr. Munk. He told us how he got the nickname "chipmunk", and how he met his wife Dorothy, who was originally from England. I even got my picture taken with him for my scrapbook. Sometimes he feels just like my grandpa instead of my doctor!

On our way home, mom and I did a little shopping for brace-friendly clothes for the next school year, which was starting in only three weeks. Mom let me drive on the turnpike, which was the first time I had driven since May 19!

In early August I came back to make the mold for my new back brace. Then I had to wait two weeks for it to be finished. That would be just as school resumed. I suddenly realized that summer was nearly over and I felt as if I didn't really get a summer break yet.

My new brace was made of two pieces and when I tried it on, it seemed smaller and fit so much better than my previous brace. Even so, a few adjustments were necessary so we were told to leave and come back in two hours. Mom and I went school shopping for school supplies for Annie and me. I found everything but a much needed book bag.

The brace fit great and I was so happy because it was less bulky! Dr. Munk was a bit disappointed because I still leaned slightly to the right in it, but he was pleased with how my incision was healing. I was already wearing a ¼ inch lift in my shoe, but he suggested we get a ½ inch lift built in that shoe because with my right leg being somewhat shorter than my left it would help me straighten out over time. The x-rays showed that my spine was quite straight. Afterwards mom and I went to get a new pair of walking shoes that had a bigger sole so a ½ inch lift could be fitted.

August 21st started out as a usual day. I made lunch for dad, Annie and me and then I went with my friend Rebekah to volunteer at the hospital. We worked all afternoon in the radiology department, which was our favorite department and we enjoyed the people who worked there. I made supper for my family that night and we were just relaxing that evening while dad was in the basement repairing our washer. Suddenly he came running up the stairs and his hand was bleeding profusely. Mom quickly wrapped it up in a towel and off they went to the hospital.

While waiting to hear back from them, I cleaned the blood off of the walls and kitchen floor and the basement room where he had been working. It looked like a murder scene! Mom soon called and said they were on their way to the University of Toledo Medical Center because they couldn't stop the bleeding. Dad got 16 stitches in his hand that night and he and mom came home around 5 am after an exhausting night. That was another long night. We were all glad that our first day of school wasn't the next day.

* * *

My junior year in high school started out well on August 23, 2006, although I was almost late to class because I couldn't get the combination in my locker to open. I found out after school that I got a job in the dietary department at a nearby nursing home, and I was so excited because I enjoy being around older people! I would be taking orders for the residents in the dining room during supper and set the room back up for breakfast.

My back was steadily becoming more painful when I took the brace off and I leaned more to my right. My doctors said I needed to wait to see if my back would straighten out naturally with time. Dr. Munk said I could start running at the beginning of 2007. That was good news because I wanted to get back to training for cross country, and I enjoyed running.

When I was at school, I really never thought about my back. I had a lot of activities and I was trying to excel in class and make good grades. I volunteered at the hospital once a week and sometimes more. I worked for a catering business on the weekends, and now I was starting my new job. I spent time with my dog, horses, and bottle-feeding my baby calves. I was also an FFA reporter for my school which meant I had to keep the chapter scrapbook current and write articles for the local newspapers about our chapter's activities. I really enjoyed all of my classes and schoolmates.

In November we had a day off because of parent teacher conferences. My friend Rebekah and I were up at 7am and on our way to our local hospital where we changed into scrubs, foot covers, hairs covers, and face masks. We were observing surgery that day with an orthopedic surgeon, and this time I was on the other side of the operating table!

We saw five surgeries that day. Before each surgery, the surgeon would explain to us what he was going to do and during the surgery he would often describe in great detail what he was doing so we could understand what was happening. We saw an endoscopy surgery on a man's shoulder to fix his broken tendon, and then two elbow surgeries followed by an ACL (anterior cruciate ligament) surgery on a knee. That was the most interesting to me. A hamstring was removed, cleaned, and then used to fix the torn ACL. The last surgery was for a torn meniscus in the knee. It was a long, but very interesting day, and we were excited to have seen so many surgeries.

The next day I was back to see Dr. Munk and an orthotic specialist because I was being casted for another mold for a back brace that would hold me in place better than the brace I already had. My sister, Annie came along to watch, since she'd heard all about my previous casting stories. As he worked, Dr. Munk explained how my "mind's eye" still thought that I was standing straight even when I was l crooked and I needed to retrain the muscles in my back. He thought I needed to be patient and give my back more time.

Two weeks later my new brace was finished and we went back to try it out. I was a bit disappointed because it was similar to the earlier one and I liked my two piece brace better. After it was fitted, we saw Dr. Munk. He was very pleased with how straight I was in my new brace and had new x-rays done with my brace on. But he took one look at the x-ray and it was clear he wasn't happy. The vertebrae right below my rods, at the L4 level, tilted slightly to the right, which may have been why I leaned to my right when standing up.

Dr. Munk was totally puzzled. He asked for new x-rays to be taken when I was sitting and lying down, without the brace. From his findings, I needed to have another surgery. He told us that in all his 35 years of being an orthopedic surgeon, he had only had two spine cases (including me) when he had to operate again after a spinal fusion, and I'm the only one who needed a third surgery.

It was Thanksgiving weekend, so we couldn't make any appointments, but Dr. Munk wanted me to see the orthopedic surgeon in Ann Arbor, Michigan for his opinion, and have another EMG done so he could discuss with other doctors about the best treatment options for my spine. We were at his office for quite a long time, and as mom and I drove home, we wondered what the future was going to hold. That night during my devotions, I came across a verse from Psalm 18:28-29 that gave me comfort. *"You, O Lord, keep my lamp burning; my God turns my darkness into light. With Your help I can advance against a troop; with my God I can scale a wall."* With all the disappointments, there were always many blessings, which I felt were God's way of turning my darkness into light and negative situations into positive ones. I had met so many wonderful and encouraging people along my journey.

The following week mom stopped by at Dr. Munk's office to pick up the x-rays to take with us when we met with the orthopedist in Ann Arbor again.

Dr. Munk came out to talk with her and said that he was waiting to make any major decisions until he heard back from the orthopedist. Depending on what he would say, Dr. Munk would decide whether to send us to St. Louis, Missouri to another orthopedic surgeon for his opinion. So nothing was cast in stone yet but I was so appreciative of how quickly I was able to get appointments scheduled.

> *"Consider it pure joy, my brothers, whenever you face trials*
> *of many kinds, because you know that the testing of your*
> *faith develops perseverance." James 1:2-3 (NIV)*

The next day dad, mom, and I went to see the orthopedist. After examining me he told us he wanted the chief of orthopedic surgery to see me, but first, he wanted new x-rays of my spine taken while I was standing without my brace on. Later that afternoon with x-rays in hand, we saw the chief pediatric orthopedic surgeon who saw from the x-rays that my spine was out of line by 20 centimeters from top to bottom. That was quite a surprise to everyone. I knew I was leaning but I didn't think I was over that much.

Both doctors agreed that surgery was the only option for my case but they weren't sure what should be done. They requested a myelogram, which is similar to a spinal tap, because the surgeon said that the instrumentation along my spine made the MRI photos blurry. They wanted to be sure that my spinal cord wasn't at all affected. They told us they would be in touch with Dr. Munk with their opinions and said they were going to present my case to the board of orthopedic surgeons to see if they had any suggestions.

Again we left with no answers – if anything, only more questions! We had been at the hospital for five hours and with a two hour drive back home, I would miss another day at school. Luckily my teachers were very understanding and kept me caught up.

Many nights I enjoyed listening to a few worship songs before falling asleep to help me relax. In the midst of dealing with my physical pain and frustrations, I found hope and comfort in God's presence. Some turn away from their faith in difficulties but I found that my relationship with God grew in ways that I never could have imagined. I had read the Bible for many years but now it seemed to come alive in my life.

I had the myelogram the following week at Toledo Hospital. There was a bit of a problem when they tried to put in the IV. Unfortunately, I was so dehydrated that my veins kept collapsing. That was the first time I almost passed out from a needle. I had been watching my nurse wiggle the needle around in my hand until I got really hot and everything became very fuzzy. So instead of using an IV relaxant medication they gave me a pill to help. I figured that after two major spine surgeries, I could deal with this one needle poke.

The shot to numb the area of my spine stung a bit but then I barely felt the needle injecting the dye into my spinal canal. At one point I think the doctor hit a nerve because I felt a tingling sensation that went down my whole left leg and made it jump. While I was on the same table they took some 3D x-rays with a machine that rotated around me and then they wheeled me to the CT scanner room. The CT scan showed where the dye was in my spine. If there was any problem area, that spot would stay white, but if my spinal cord was normal, it would remain black. The CT scan showed that everything appeared normal.

In mid December, Dr. Munk called us in to his office to talk about our upcoming appointment with the orthopedic surgeon in St Louis and what might happen, depending on the surgeon's findings. We had a great visit and also took some homemade Christmas candy with us for Dr. Munk and his staff to nibble on. We left in good spirits and did a bit of Christmas shopping on our way home.

Christmas came and it rained. No snow, just rain. Our weather in Ohio can certainly be unpredictable. It just didn't feel like Christmas without snow and I felt so guilty getting gifts from my parents when I knew they had plenty of medical bills to pay because of me.

**Excerpt from journal. *Jesus, I love You so much and I long to be a light for You among the people I see and come in contact with. Jesus, this world is hungry for the truth. I am Your messenger God, please use me in Your mighty ways for I long for everyone to know You. You are my light in darkness, and my rainbow during a storm. You are my hope. I don't know how people live their lives daily without You. I pray that my life will be an offering for You. I was put here on earth for a purpose! I am Your servant!* **

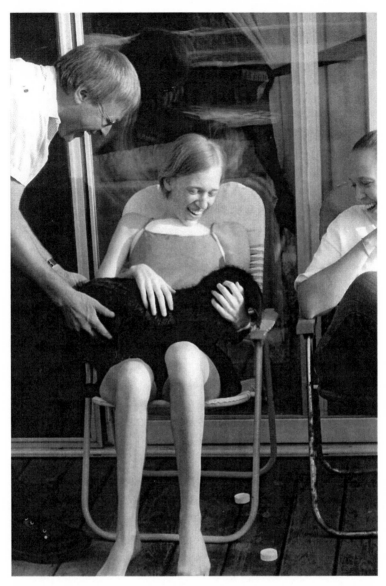

A day after I came home from the hospital after my second surgery, my whole family came over which I found suspicious. I was told to sit on the deck and close my eyes. To my surprise, dad placed something fuzzy and squirmy in my lap. I got a labradoodle puppy for my birthday! He was my therapy dog because I had to get up multiple times during the day to take him for short walks.

7

Taking a 50/50 chance

When I said, "My foot is slipping," Your love, O Lord, supported me. When anxiety was great within me, Your consolation brought joy to my soul. Psalm 94:18-19 (NIV)

On January 7, 2007 we were on our way to St. Louis, Missouri. I drove part of the way, which for me, made the eight hour trip seem shorter.

Our appointment with the orthopedic surgeon was early the next morning, and when I woke up, I was extremely nervous. When we arrived at the hospital we were told to go straight to the x-ray department first. With my new x-rays in hand, we headed back to the orthopedic surgeons office. In many hallways I felt like I was walking inside a five star hotel and not a hospital.

The nurse hung up many of my previous x-rays in my exam room, along with the ones just taken. It looked just like a small museum in there with the walls covered with x-rays of my spine taken from different angles. After she was done, the doctor walked in.

After asking many questions about my medical history, the surgeon asked me to stand up, walk, and jump up and down. Then I laid down on my back and he measured my leg lengths and checked my reflexes. Then I rolled over on to my stomach and he prodded, massaged, and shifted my spine. Then he asked for me to have more x-rays before we left.

So we went back to the x-ray department where they took x-rays while I was sitting with my brace both on and off, and then while lying sideways and on my back. By the time I walked out to the waiting room, my parents were wondering what I had been doing back there because it took so long!

After the surgeon looked at the newest x-rays he told us that I needed another surgery to fuse one more of my vertebrae in my lumbar spine because it was leaning or tilting to the right. If that surgery didn't work, he thought my whole spine should be fused down to my sacrum. He also suggested that Dr. Munk put me under general anesthesia to see how much movement my spine had when my body was completely relaxed. Our 8:30am appointment had turned into 5½ hours long, but we felt as if we had some answers.

With the rest of the afternoon we decided to take the tram to the top of the Gateway Arch. Although we had done the same thing two years earlier on a family trip, it was still amazing to look out of the windows at the top. The sky was fairly clear, so we had a great view, but it was so windy that the arch swayed, and that was creepy. The next day we were on our way home.

When we got back I was tired from our quick trip and, on top of my medical stress, I had to study for exams at school. I've never been very good at taking exams - my nerves seem to get the best of me even when I'm well prepared and know most of the information!

It was simply a difficult time for me at school. Even though basketball is a big sport at our school I hardly ever went to the games because the students often pounded on the bleachers with their feet. Besides, I was generally exhausted after a day at school and ready for bed soon after supper. As much as I didn't want to have another surgery, I was ready to do anything to stand straight again and enjoy the activities that I used to do.

Through that period I was so grateful to the many - family, friends, and people within our church and the community - who continued to send me cards and support my family in so many ways. Simply sending a card seems like such a small gesture but it can make a big impact in someone's life. There were days when the cards were an answer to prayer as I needed a little encouragement. People I didn't even know sent me cards.

Towards the end of January we went back to Toledo Hospital to follow through with the St Louis surgeon's suggestion that they test my spine while I'm totally relaxed under general anesthesia. Dr. Munk and his colleague performed the test. They lifted me up while a long x-ray board was placed under me. Then they took an x-ray while I was lying down before I was put to sleep so they could compare it with the ones taken when I was in a completely relaxed state. They also planned to "cast" me while I was asleep to help stabilize my spine more than in the brace.

It was really strange as I started to wake up. I knew I was in the casting room and I could hear everyone, but I couldn't respond because there was still a tube in my throat. I heard them saying that I was not taking deep enough breaths, and Dr. Munk was telling me to take deep breaths and wake up, which I really tried to do, but I couldn't. Eventually, after I did wake up my parents came to the recovery room and both doctors got me up to walk and they were puzzled because I was very straight when sedated but leaned when I stood. Dr. Munk trimmed the cast down a little and asked me to walk up and down the hallway for him. Then they said it was enough for the day. It was 8:30 at night. What a day that was! As soon as I got home, I was in bed and out like a light.

The next day my parents let me sleep in and go to school at lunchtime because I was exhausted and so sore. My principal was understanding about my situation since he had had four vertebrae fused the previous summer. He remembered the pain after his surgery and told me he had no idea how I was able to manage it with so many more vertebrae fused. I so appreciated his understanding and I felt an even greater respect for him because we shared something in common that even my friends didn't really understand.

The new cast was very uncomfortable and I leaned more in that than in my brace making me become self-conscious so that Friday we saw Dr. Munk, who decided to cut it off. Afterwards, he took some pictures of me with his camera, and had more x-rays taken. He told us he would e-mail the most recent pictures to the surgeon in St. Louis, and talk with his colleague as well. He thought we couldn't wait much longer because my spine was continuing to deteriorate. He wanted to set a date for surgery within the next month or so when he and his colleague could operate together. He put me back on iron pills to start building up my red blood cells so I could donate blood when I got a surgery date.

February 8, 2007, was not a good day. It was really cold and windy outside that morning so dad went over to feed the horses. He found my beloved One-Across on the frozen ground, dead. The night before I had had a great time with both horses and I had spent time grooming each one while watching the sunset. I never saw any sign that either one of them wasn't well. Many people we talked with thought she probably died from colic, which is when the horses' intestines twist, because it happened so fast. If so, at least she didn't suffer too long. Dad cut a lock of One-Across' mane for me before she was taken away.

One-Across had definitely lived a long and great life and I was grateful that I got to spend her last few months with her, even if she did like to chew on the barn and steal Farah's food. I felt bad for Farah because she was all alone in her pasture again.

That night after school mom told me I was scheduled for surgery on Friday, March 2. That was only three weeks away. I was relieved that something was going to be done but I knew how the pain would be afterwards. And now I couldn't go on our high school choir trip to Nashville, Tennessee. I went out to groom Farah because I always felt better when I was over there and I think she knew when I needed to talk and be with her too.

* * *

Valentine's Day soon came. School was canceled for two days due to a bad snowstorm. I got up in the middle of the night and hid little bags of candy and cards I had made for everyone in my family for Valentine's Day, and for supper, dad made us a huge heart pizza with little heart breadsticks. They were so delicious and special!

The next day I donated blood and afterward mom and I went shopping for a prom dress because after my surgery I'd be in a cast until a few days before prom. At the first store, I found the perfect dress and no other dress we saw that day could compare with it. It was a light blue color, strapless, with sequins on the top and a low criss-cross back. (I wanted to find a dress that had an open back so that I could show off my scar nicely). I was assuming the surgery would work so I bought a dress that I couldn't wear my brace underneath.

School was becoming very stressful for me because I was trying to get work done ahead of time. We had a day off on President's Day so we went to see Dr. Munk so he could talk with us about the surgery and answer our questions. He said the surgery could give me a chance of becoming straighter or it could make it worse - it was 50/50 chance. I would probably have to stay in the hospital for at least three days. If it didn't work, it would be quite awhile until they could do anything else because he would want to try every option before fusing all of the vertebrae. If they had to do that, it would be a long recovery and I wouldn't have much mobility or flexibility in my back anymore, so I was really hoping this next surgery would work.

The next day, school was canceled again because of fog. That was a lucky break because I had to write a 1200 word paper in Spanish by mid March and I was so happy to get a head start on it before surgery.

That afternoon we went back to Toledo Hospital for my pre- admission appointment. The physician's assistant was so personable that I told her I wanted to be a nurse someday. She was so excited and took time to tell me about her 40 years of working in the health care field and she gave me a lot of tips for colleges and nursing in general. It was great to hear her views and made me more excited about my future.

* * *

On the day before my surgery I was stressed with trying to get my homework done and then I got a note during class saying that mom would be picking me up after school for a doctor's appointment. I was so tired of doctor appointments! Luckily I was able to spend time alone in the school greenhouse that afternoon while I worked on my agriculture project on asexual propagation with different types of plants. As I prepared small cuttings from parent plants and put the cuttings in the soil to see if they would regenerate in a few days, I thought about many things and I closed my eyes and prayed in a way that I've never prayed before. I was pouring myself out to God and trying not to cry because I was still at school. That was when it hit me; I felt extremely calm and as if I was dreaming. I saw myself walking out of an airplane (that part was a little blurry), but I could see myself very clearly. I was walking, and I was straight, with no help of a brace, and smiling. If that didn't bring me back to my senses, I don't know what would.

I felt calm, reassured, and ready to face whatever was thrown my way. Yet I still had a sinking feeling deep inside that something was going to happen, but I couldn't pinpoint what. I went to my last two classes of the day, but I couldn't really focus.

Then school was over and mom was out in the parking lot waiting for me, so we headed to Toledo to see Dr. Munk. I still had a lot of homework to do and three big projects that I had to complete before surgery - only 1½ days to go.

Dr. Munk explained that he wanted me to come in for one more x-ray. He asked me to lie down on my back and he put his knee in my left side and pulled me over to the left as much as he could. It was very painful and he did it twice but we got the job done and he was pleased with the final x-ray. He then said that after surgery he would put me in a cast that would extend down to my right knee. The purpose was to keep that side of my body straight and prevent me from bending my knee because that was a coping mechanism for me and helped with the pain.

Dr. Munk said he would like his colleague to see me also. They asked me to lie down on my stomach, and they massaged my lower back to relax my muscles because they thought the muscles in my lower back might be having spasms. They both left the room to confer and when they came back they were talking as if we should explore other options before we go ahead with surgery. Mom was upset and I started crying, which I never do, but I just couldn't help it because I was already quite stressed. I told them that I couldn't take the pain and fatigue that came with my back much longer. They thought perhaps I should see another neurologist, and talked about giving me Botox treatments in my lower back to relax the muscles that looked like they were spasming. This made me frustrated because I had already seen neurologists who had said that after much testing, I didn't have a neurological problem but an orthopedic one.

Both doctors then emphasized the fact that there was a fifty percent chance that my spine would get worse with the surgery and they kept throwing the question around about how, "is it really worth it to undergo another major surgery when we don't know what the end result will be?" But then they talked from the other angle, about how this surgery could help a little or quite a great deal. In the end, they left the decision up to me because they said it was my body that would be affected.

After considering it for quite awhile I decided I wanted to go ahead with the surgery as we had originally planned, but I would let them know if I changed my mind. I just wanted to be straight again, although I knew this surgery might not work.

My simple little appointment for some x-rays turned into an ordeal that lasted several hours. So much for getting my homework and projects finished that night. We said our goodbyes to everyone and walked to our car. Mom and I just sat in there for awhile, talking and crying, which with the stress we were dealing with, is just what we needed to do.

It was nearly 10:00 at night and my poor dad was worried because we were so late getting home. I got right into bed because school would come bright and early in the morning. **Excerpt from journal. *Jesus, I love You and thank You so much for embracing me when times are difficult. Jesus, You are the reason I am alive and breathing. There are so many stumbling blocks throughout life, but that is really our time to shine, our time to show the devil that nothing can come in between our relationship, Jesus. You are everything to me.* **

A Mother's Perspective

I was at work just a few days before Libbey's 3rd surgery, and the plan was to fuse more vertebrae in hopes of eliminating the "lean" that continued to worsen.

The phone rang and it was Helen, Dr. Munk's nurse calling to ask if I could bring Libbey in after work for a couple routine x-rays, so they would have some more pre-op "pictures." No problem I told her, so when I was finished for the day, I picked Libbey up from school and we drove to Toledo to have the x-rays taken.... no big deal, we had traveled this road hundreds of times it seemed.

It soon turned into a "nightmare" appointment with not only x-rays taken, but doubts expressed as to whether the surgery would be beneficial.....or not... after Dr. Munk's colleague examined her. Before we left, they told Libbey to decide what she thought was the "right" thing to do and if she felt she still wanted to have the surgery done.....or to wait a bit longer. She ultimately decided for the surgery and we supported her. The surgery did help.....for about 6 months when things began to worsen....again.

I didn't sleep well that night, or the next. I was still questioning whether or not I should have the surgery and couldn't figure out the best solution. The day before surgery I turned in most of my homework assignments, except for my math. In my last period English class, five other girls and myself had to do a presentation about a book we recently read together as a group. It actually went fairly smoothly, especially since I made cookies to keep everyone's mouth busy, even though we did it a few days early because I would be gone.

During the afternoon announcements our principal said, "Tomorrow a strong young lady by the name of Libbey Eicher will be undergoing another back surgery." He told everyone to keep me in their thoughts and prayers throughout the next couple of days as I recovered from surgery. I didn't know he was going to do that and I was kind of embarrassed, but it was very thoughtful of him!

When the day ended many people came up to me and said that they would be thinking and praying for me. The support I received was overwhelming! I stopped to talk with my good friends, Rebekah and Chelsea, and then remembered that my mom was picking me up. I walked down with them to our school lobby and then pretended that I forgot something in my locker, so I could go back upstairs.

I had bought a pack of candy and a card to put in Rebekah's locker because she had been so encouraging and a good friend through this whole ordeal.

When I got to the car one of my former gym teachers was talking with my mom. He gave me a very nice card and told us that we'd be in his thoughts and prayers. Within his card he gave me a copy of his daily devotional book that talked about courage and how whatever challenge we are faced with, God can handle it. I really needed to read that. The past week had brought on a rollercoaster of emotions for me, but God was in control and would see me through yet another surgery no matter what the outcome would be.

I spent a long time that evening grooming Farah because I knew it'd be a few days before I'd see her again. I always liked to sit on the fence while watching the sunset and listening to Farah chew her supper. It was so peaceful over with her.

Later my parents took Annie to Katie and Derek's house. She gave me a quick hug and then left quickly because she looked like she was going to cry. We all tried to get to bed early that night even though sleep was difficult. I did find comfort in reading the Bible and praying.

Excerpt from my journal. *Heavenly Father, my life is in Your hands. I know that You never give us more than we can't handle, and when we are exhausted, You reach out to us with both physical and spiritual rest. Knowing You, Jesus, is the best think that has ever happened to me. The difficulties in my life have opened my eyes even more to Your love and has deepened my walk with You, Lord.*

8 Surgery #3

"No matter how little we can change about our circumstances, we always have a choice about our attitude toward the situation."
Vonette Bright

The next day, March 2nd, we were up at 3:30 a.m. Butterflies were already awake in my stomach. ***Good morning Libbey, this is God! I will be handling all your problems today. I will not need your help--so have a good day!*** As I woke up, this was the quote I saw on my wall. This was a reminder that neither the doctors nor I had everything under control, only God did. I took a shower and packed some last minute things. It was quite an early morning but I think my adrenaline was really pumping because I didn't feel very tired even though I'd hardly slept. Before we left, mom and dad came into my room and we prayed together before the hustle and bustle of the hospital.

We left an hour later, mom in their car, and dad and I following in my car with me driving. It was very cold outside, but the sky was clear, and we could see the stars shining above us. The turnpike was clear of traffic and so was Toledo. Not many people are out and about that early!

It took just over an hour to get to the hospital and had no problem parking our cars side by side. There were other families with patients in the waiting room by the time we arrived, but I was the youngest, again.

Soon after six they took us all back and I had the same pre-op room that I'd had six weeks earlier when I got casted under general anesthesia, and I also had the same wonderful nurse I had had the previous times.

When I was prepped they allowed my sisters and brother in law to come back to see me. Everyone looked a little ragged around the edges due to the early morning but we had a very good time talking and laughing quietly together. Helen also poked her head in to say hello. I really felt better knowing she was going to be with me until I was put under general anesthesia.

Dr. Munk then came back and said hello to the whole family and he said he would be putting the cast on me when he finished the surgery that day and it would extend to my right knee. It was a relief to know I'd still be asleep when I was casted this time.

Once again, we stopped at the kiss corner, where everyone in my family gave me a hug and a kiss. I then went through those big, double "personnel only" doors. Helen, my surgical nurse, and I waited outside the OR for a bit because it wasn't quite ready and suddenly felt a little woozy and more relaxed. They had inserted some sedative medication into my IV without me knowing it. Very sneaky!

Then I was wheeled in and placed beside the surgical table. Those three huge surgical lights loomed above me, ready to do their job. The anesthesiologist held an oxygen mask above my nose and mouth, and I was told to take deep breaths.

Around 3:30 that afternoon I was taken to the recovery room. It seems the pain medicine caused me to stop breathing and so I was put on a ventilator for a while until I could breathe on my own. I remember hearing Dr. Munk, my nurses, and my parents talking, but I was still unconscious, which proves hearing really is the last sense to leave your body. One of the nurses was telling a funny story and although I wasn't awake, I recounted the story to my parents a few days later and we had a good chuckle from it.

I was wheeled to the pediatric ICU but I honestly don't remember very much from Friday to Sunday just that, whenever I did wake up, I was in unbearable pain. Nurses would come then and give me wonderful pain medication or something to help me sleep. It was easier for me and my family if I could sleep through those first few days.

I remember that two players from the Toledo Storm hockey team came to visit me on Sunday night. I still have their autographed season book but, to this day, I can't figure out from their signatures which of them came (and my eyes were closed so I don't know if they were cute or not).

On Monday morning two guys called the "lift team" held all my IV lines and my catheter and lifted me into an upright position. Dad was at the end of the bed to hold me up and I had to stay like that for five minutes. It seemed like forever! It felt like the cast was grinding right into my lower back. I clung to dad and moaned and cried the whole time because I was in so much pain.

Then the lift guys gently lifted me back to bed. They came back numerous times that day.

A Father's Perspective

The worst part is after surgery. The pain is just horrible for me to watch. After this surgery, I was told to help hold her up while she stood for five minutes. Holding her there with tears streaming down her cheeks was the hardest thing I ever did. She was in such great pain but yet I was holding her tight to me, next to my heart, which really felt good .

I was exhausted. When visitors came I listened but with my eyes closed because my eyes felt like lead. My pastor came to visit in the late afternoon, and then another very nice couple from my church came. Soon after they left, my high school principal came in to see me. With all he had to do, he came out of his way to come visit, which really meant a lot to me.

Later that evening, several high school all star football players from the Northwest Ohio area came into the ICU and visited with all the patients. They gave each of us a foam football to keep. I was a little self conscious of how I looked because there were many very nice looking guys my age stopping by and I hadn't had my hair washed in days and had no makeup on!

Tuesday morning, my ICU nurses came by and said they were going to give me a "fluff n buff" bath and make me squeaky clean. They didn't use the normal hospital soap; they used Bath and Body Works shampoo, conditioner, and body wash. I was certainly pampered! They finished me off by rubbing good smelling cream on my arms and legs. They did a great job, and I know my whole room smelled so good! My nasogastric tube was taken out also, which felt so nice on my throat.

In the early afternoon Dr. Munk and the orthotic specialist I had seen before, worked some magic and cut some of the cast off from around my upper thigh and put on a hinge which connected the cast from my hip to my leg so I could sit down. When I would be standing, the hinge would then lock so that I would be standing straight and unable to bend my knee. This process was painful because they were constantly rolling me around but I was glad that I would then be able to sit down. Without the hinge I would have had to either stand or lay down, so I was so grateful to them for this new idea.

When they were done and my cast was completely dried, Dr. Munk helped me stand up by myself for the first time since surgery and then he held onto me and helped me walk around the room. The cast still felt like it was grinding into my back. It was like I was dragging myself and leaning on him for support. Walking would really take some getting used to with the cast on.

That night, my sisters came to visit and brought get well balloons for me. During their visit I was wheeled to the regular pediatric floor, with my family there to cheer me on and make me laugh.

Later that week a physical therapist came in and showed me some strengthening exercises to do and I was given a walker to help me do my exercises and get around. The activities director brought a TV into my room so mom and I watched the funny Ice Age 1 movie. It hurt to laugh, so I had to be careful. I should have picked a sad movie instead.

Bright and early Thursday morning, I had a PICC (central) line placed in my upper arm so I could be given my TPN and lipids since I wasn't able to eat much. TPN is specially mixed up by the pharmacy each morning with the nutrients that a patient needs. Each patient's needs are different. The doctor numbed my upper arm and made a small incision and then inserted a small blue tube into a vein which then went directly into my heart from where the nutrients could be taken in and absorbed much faster. Whenever my blood was drawn, it could also be taken out of my PICC line so now I didn't have to be poked every day. Fantastic!

On Friday I had my last therapy session where I had to show them that I could walk up and down stairs when the hinge connecting my hip to my thigh was locked. This wasn't too difficult but I did have to really concentrate. That night my sister and dad took me for a long walk, and it felt good. At bedtime all of my IVs were disconnected which meant that I could sleep the whole night through without interruptions.

On Saturday afternoon, March 10, Dr. Munk came in, and by the way he was talking, I didn't think he was going to discharge me. I still wasn't eating enough, but I was itching to get out of the hospital. After much talking with mom and me, he decided to discharge me, and I was so happy. He took out my PICC line, which was really long, and my mom signed the discharge papers. I was even allowed to walk down to the main lobby with mom and wait for her to bring the car to the main entrance. I got home that afternoon to a happy family and an excited dog. I sure missed those sloppy kisses!

The days went by slowly as I recuperated at home. I worked on my scrap book and did crossword puzzles. My appetite was still not the greatest, but better than the previous summer. The cast prevented me from eating very much because of the pressure that it put on my chest and back. After three weeks, I was glad to go back to school. It had been cold and snowy outside so I had been staying inside all day and was really feeling cooped up. Mom had been picking up my homework but without specific instructions I had no idea how to do half of it, and so I wanted to get back to school before I got too far behind.

My first day back at school went fairly smoothly and many people stopped to welcome me back and ask how I was feeling. It made me feel kind of weird because I was still the same person I had been before I left to have surgery, but I appreciated their concern. I just stayed half days that first week until my body was a little stronger.

I attended the annual FFA banquet the next night because as the FFA reporter I had many roles to play. I so wanted to make it to the banquet which was one of my main goals before my surgery. With my cast on, I had to wear my sweatpants instead of the traditional black skirt, but at least I was there! With my heavy cast, I was so hot in the stuffy gymnasium that was full of people; I felt as if I was cooking so after we ate, mom and I took a walk outside to cool me down before the program started.

My teachers really helped me catch up with the homework and the lessons that I had missed and a few just canceled the homework I missed. That took a big weight off of my shoulders.

I was taking chemistry at the time and this subject builds up as the year goes on. So I had to make up the worksheets, which were quite confusing. I had a great teacher who helped me after school for a few days to gain an understanding of what I needed to learn. For a few days I even ate lunch with my math teacher while he helped me understand the homework. I was so grateful for their help.

Excerpt from my journal. *Father God, You have stood by us and never leave! No matter where we are, or what we are doing, You are right next to us holding us up no matter what situation we are in. I am so grateful to know You as my personal Savior and I love knowing that wherever I go, You go also. You are always holding me in Your loving arms. Sweet, Jesus, I love You more than anything in this world. You are my everything in life!*

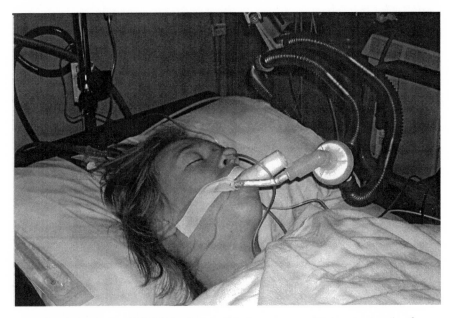

On March 2, 2007 I had my third surgery which consisted of extending my fusion down one more vertebrae in hopes of getting me to stand straight again. After the surgery I was also casted down to my right knee. That night I needed to be on the ventilator for a little while until I was able to breathe on my own again.

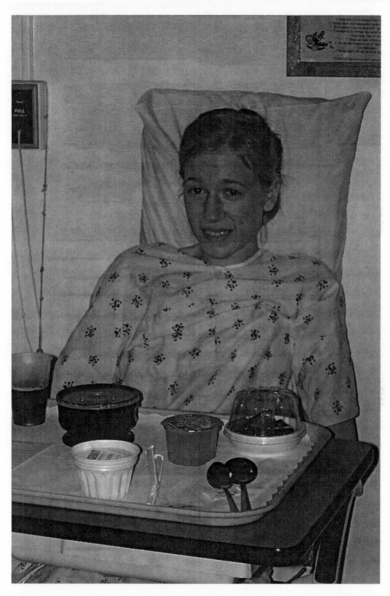

After every surgery, I hardly ever had an appetite, but when the dinner trays came I had to sit in a chair and at least look at my food, in hopes that maybe I might take a few bites.

9 Hip Bones and a Million Bucks

Be still, and in the quiet moments, listen to the voice of your Heavenly Father. His words can renew your spirit - no one knows you and your needs like He does." Janet L. Weaver Smith

My post op appointment with Dr. Munk started with a question from the nurses about whether I had a date for prom yet, and I had to say no. During the weeks I was out of school it seems everyone had asked each other to prom, which was disappointing. My friend and I had just decided we'd go together without dates and have just as much fun. Many at the office joked that Dr. Munk should go with me to prom. Dr. Munk's wife, Dorothy, who was a nurse, chuckled and said he'd have a great time, though he was a bit of a "rough dancer," which gave us all a good laugh!

Dr. Munk came in and wondered what all the commotion was in my room since we were all laughing! He analyzed me standing in my cast, and then sent me to x-ray. He wasn't pleased by what he saw on x-rays because my spine was still tilting to the right, but not nearly as much as before surgery. He told us that they had casted me, after surgery, to the point that I was standing slightly to my left. This was very disappointing news and I think they thought the surgery was not successful because, if I was leaning in my cast, I would probably lean when it came off. I still had a strong hope that I would stand straight when the cast came off.

They didn't cut the cast off but they did cut it around my incision so Dr. Munk could take the dressing off and check my incision. He said it was healing perfectly and told me I could begin to drive and go back to working, which made me very happy! Afterwards mom and I drove to see the orthotic specialist to have measurements taken of my right leg so that he could add a right leg cuff with a hinge to my brace.

On our way home we stopped at the mall for me buy another pair of sweatpants because that was all I could wear with my cast on. Sometimes you just need to buy something new to make you feel pretty, and that's just what I needed because the cast made me feel so bulky and as if I had big hips!

"Therefore we do not lose heart. Though outwardly we are wasting away, yet inwardly we are being renewed day by day. So let us fix our eyes not on what is seen, but on what is unseen. For what is seen is temporary, but what is unseen is eternal."

2 Corinthians 4:16, 18 (NIV)

Two weeks later over Easter break, I volunteered again with my friend at the Fulton County Health Center. We had to get up early to be in surgery on time with our blue scrubs, caps, masks, and booties. We were observing surgery with the orthopedic surgeon again!

This time we observed two hip replacement surgeries. My friend and I even got to feel an actual hip bone after it was removed. Not many people can say they've held a human hip bone! I'm amazed how body parts can be replaced and then lives are lived like they were before, only without pain.

Finally, on April 11, my cast was cut off. After much sawing and cutting, they finally got it off. I was getting worried that I'd have to stay in it permanently! I stood up, and was surprisingly straight. I still leaned slightly to the right, but even Dr. Munk was surprised and said I looked much better. I felt so free without the heavy cast and I was so ready to take a shower!

I was also happy to report to the office staff that I had gotten a date for prom. Rebekah and I had managed to persuade two good friends of ours, Matt and Michael, to go with us to prom. The guys weren't even planning to go to prom, but we worked hard to convince them and they took our advice!

Dr. Munk put my cast back on with elastic bandages around the outside, and then we went to pick up and try on my new brace from Cole Orthotics. We then drove back to Dr. Munk's office so he could see me in my brace. Dr. Munk found that the hinge connecting my brace to the leg cuff was bent in a way that was causing me to lean to the right, so he bent it to the left and I put it back on and walked up and down the hallway so that he could make sure it was correctly bent. I was standing straighter.

"Be joyful always; pray continually; give thanks in all circumstances, for this is God's will for you in Christ Jesus."

1 Thessalonians 5:16-18 (NIV)

* * *

April 14, prom day, I was up bright and early, so excited to get all dressed up! My friend, Rebekah, came over around 10am, and we drove to the florist to pick up our flowers. Then it was time for our hairdresser appointment. We had both decided to wear our hair half down and really curly and I brought an orange daisy for my hair stylist to put in my hair to add a nice soft touch.

It was a historic day in our community because there was a huge fire in the downtown buildings of Wauseon early that morning and there were still 28 fire departments there (including my brother-in-law Derek, a volunteer rescue and fireman) when we arrived for our appointment. The hair salon was just down the street a little ways so with all of the activity in the area it was very difficult to find parking.

I spent the afternoon working on my homework and scrapbook so I wouldn't mess up my hair. Later I put in my contacts and put on my makeup. Then I slipped into my beautiful blue dress. I felt like a million bucks. After being stuck in my cast for so long, I felt pretty and girly again!

Around 5pm Rebekah came over and our dates, Matt and Michael arrived to pick us up. We put corsages on each other (which was quite the experience), and then my parents took some pictures. We were then off to the country club for dinner.

It was snowing heavily all the way and it was hard to see anything. Then we realized nobody remembered to bring the directions along, so we got lost and had to stop three times to ask for directions. We were the last couples to arrive, which was both embarrassing and amusing because everyone was waiting on us to eat dinner.

After dinner, we drove back to the high school for the dance. The snow that night was almost magical. I felt gorgeous in my dress and we had fun. It was a night I'll never forget.

My date will probably never know how much he made my night at prom. All through my last surgery my real incentive was to be able to go to prom and be standing straight. Everything I hoped for that night really did come true.

A Sister's (Katie) Perspective

Derek had a fire call very early that morning and left in my car. He called around 5:30 to tell me that downtown Wauseon was on fire. I called Dad to confirm the news and he said all of the area fire departments were there.

Fearing the worse for my car (Derek had cleaned it up the night before so it would be looking sharp for you to take to prom), I assumed we would have to figure out a plan B for the evening. But just then Grandpa called to see if I needed a ride to pick up the car because it looked like Derek would be on call for most of the day. To help you out, I decided to suck it up and go out in public without showering or putting on make-up!

Unfortunately the car was trapped between another car and a fire truck. After numerous attempts trying to maneuver it out, Grandpa and I decided it was a lost cause. Just as we were about to walk away, a fireman came up offering to move the fire truck so we could get the car out. It was so nice of him to help us, especially because the truck belonged to a different department than he worked for. With his help, we got the car out and away from the fire equipment. Luckily for you, the car didn't smell like smoke, which was surprising because it was parked so close to the fire.

Watching you walk into the school for the prom dance, I knew all the morning's frustrations were worth it. You were beautiful that night and even though it was too cold for a prom, the snow that fell that night made the night seem so magical for you.

My teachers were great and continued to encourage and support me. A letter from one of my favorite teachers showed me that I was not alone in this journey - I had so many people helping me along the way to stay positive. *"Faced with many challenges, you have chosen to bring joy and love into the lives of all the people you encounter. God has certainly filled your heart with a "super sized" amount of love. Your courage is an inspiration for all who know you."* This teacher was a role model for me. He often stressed that we should never settle for second best because each of us has a great potential to benefit this world.

A few weeks later we went back to see Dr. Munk and I brought my prom pictures to show everyone. They would have been disappointed if I didn't. Dr. Munk asked me to walk up and down the hallway with my brace on and then without it. He was still very pleased with the progress my spine had made and he said I didn't need to come back for two months. That was a record for me!

Spring came and when I wasn't in school you could find me studying, working at Fairlawn Haven Nursing Home, grooming Farah, or working with the plants I had grown for my FFA project in our school's greenhouse. I had permed my hair and once I got used to it I really liked the curls. Exams came and went and then school was over and summer vacation began.

Since my first surgery, almost a year earlier, I had not been able to ride my beloved Farah. I spent many hours grooming and lunging her for exercise, but I was beginning to think that I should sell her to a home where she could be ridden on a regular basis. It was a hard decision to make but it didn't take long before we found a fine family for her and in mid May she was sold. The night before she left, I spent a lot of time with her and cut a lock of her mane to keep. It was difficult because she and I had been through so much together. She always seemed to know just when I needed to talk and be with her because she stood still and let me hug and brush her, and talk. I had saved my money for years in advance and I got her only after proving to my parents that I was responsible. My heart broke, but I was glad she was going to a great family where she would be loved.

My two-month check up went really well. I know everyone was relieved to see me standing so straight. My x-rays looked great and I was healing nicely. I still leaned forward slightly so Dr. Munk told me to really concentrate on standing straight and doing my strengthening exercises. It was a good visit and I was to come back in six weeks, which would be right before school began.

It was a great summer and I spent time swimming, gardening, and working. I was really working on gaining my muscle tone back so I rode my bike 16 -22 miles every night. It was a time when I could just be in my own little world and think. Sometimes I couldn't believe how far I had ridden because the time went by so fast!

In mid-August I saw Dr. Munk and he was quite happy with my progress as I was standing even straighter. He told me I could give up my brace on the first day of school, which was only a week away. While I couldn't start cross country yet, I could begin to run in half mile intervals. Every two weeks I could double the distance. It was a disappointment that I couldn't run cross country right away because it was my senior year, but I was just so happy I could start running and go without my brace during the day!

It was hard to believe I was a senior in high school. How time had flown by! I was also excited because I was going to start taking some classes at the nearby community college along with my high school classes. This was a great deal because while one is in high school, college classes are paid for by the school.

Along with school, I went to the county fair (and ate all that nutritious food!), I started putting in more hours at Fairlawn Haven, and best of all, I began running. It felt so good to be doing the things I loved to do. Of course I wasn't running as fast as I used to in years previously, but it just felt so good to get out and do it again.

On October 3 mom and I went back to see Dr. Munk. He first looked at me standing up and then he rolled up the back of my shirt. Apparently I was beginning to lean to my right again very slightly. He turned me so that my back was facing mom, and she was completely amazed, because you really couldn't tell I was leaning unless my shirt was rolled up.

He asked us if we brought my back brace because he wanted to see what I looked like with it on. I didn't like the sound of that because I really didn't want to start wearing it again. While mom went to get the brace from the car I had some x-rays taken from the front and side views. My x-rays showed I was leaning to the right significantly compared with those taken just four months previously but not as bad as before my third surgery. My heart sank because I thought I was looking so good and never noticed that I was leaning at all. Dr. Munk said I could run cross-country because it was therapeutic but I needed to start wearing my brace again during the day which was what I didn't want to hear, but was glad he caught me leaning so hopefully the brace could help with that.

My hips and armpits were so sore from being rubbed by my brace since I had gone nearly six weeks without wearing it. My classmates at school also noticed that I was wearing my brace again and were concerned and asked me questions, that many times I really didn't have answers to.

A week later, I had my first cross country meet since my sophomore year.

"…let us throw off everything that hinders and the sin that so easily entangles, and let us run with perseverance the race marked out for us." Hebrews 12:1b

The race was 3.1 miles long and I still had not run three miles in my training so it was a wakeup call for me. Luckily the meet wasn't a big deal because it didn't count for our league. It was a thrill to put on my black and white jersey with the number 406 on the back. It was really hot and windy that day and it didn't help that I was really nervous. Our whole team walked the course, and then went back to our team site, and stretched. Then it was time to run. My stomach was churning.

When the gun went off I ran as fast as I used to the first mile but soon I slowed down -I wasn't in the greatest of shape yet. The course seemed to take forever, but it helped to have my whole family and our dog there cheering me on. Halfway through the course, my coach saw me struggling and told me that I could stop at any time. I looked at him and said, "I'm not giving up now!" I think he knew me better anyways. I didn't care how I placed, I just wanted to finish.

Exhausted, I crossed the long awaited finish line. My time was five minutes slower than two years earlier but I thought I did pretty well, considering I hadn't even run three miles before the race. Right away, my back leaned to the right and my body turned into jello. I was exhausted. I couldn't support my back and I knew people were watching me.

Two days later I ran in another cross country meet and that one was my last because the season was coming to a close. I ran so much better and got a better time. It helped that there was a girl from the other team running right behind me the whole time and that kept pushing me to keep my pace up. In the end she beat me as she sprinted to the finish line.

Taking college courses while in high school is a real challenge. I was working, running, and helping with chores around the house, harvesting in the fields with dad, and then there was pumpkin carving and decorating Halloween cookies. I began to lean more to the right causing slight pain in my right hip and lower back. My mom made an appointment to see Dr. Munk the next month.

The night before my appointment, my Spanish club from school went to dinner and then to an opera. It was so much fun to get all dressed up and have a "field trip." It was a very late night so it was hard to get up in time the next morning for my appointment.

When they measured me at the doctor's office I had shrunk one inch, which meant I was really starting to lean again. Dr. Munk was completely amazed at what I looked like. He told us he did not think I had an orthopedic problem anymore but possibly a neurological one since I decompensated so rapidly again. He mentioned that it could possibly be dystonia, which is a condition when muscles contract involuntarily that can cause a body to twist in different ways.

He scheduled us to go to the Cleveland Clinic in December to see a neurologist who had already heard about my case. The weeks flew by with Thanksgiving and preparing for my exams at Northwest State Community College.

From my spiritual journal. *Jesus, when I give all the earthly things I have and my stresses and frustrations, You fill my life with Your love for others, strength* *to stand up for what I know is right, faith to express my love for You, and peace in knowing that You never leave me and are always trying to carry my burdens. Jesus, when this happens, my eyes are opened to see that there's nothing else I need anymore but You! I love You! *

* * *

On December 17, 2007 my parents and I left our house at 8am for the two and a half hour drive to the Cleveland Clinic. We had just had a bad snow storm so the roads were not good. We arrived at the clinic in plenty of time and even had time to walk around the complex. The exercise was good for us after sitting in the car for quite a while and helped the time to pass more quickly.

When it was nearly time for my appointment, we headed up to the ninth floor which was for adult neurology. The neurologist had a nice comforting smile on his face when we met. He went through my history with scoliosis and asked my parents and me a lot of questions. He checked my reflexes and did a full neurological exam. I was so nervous that even my palms were sweaty, which was a first for me. He told us he was pretty sure that I did not have dystonia but just to be sure he was going to put me on a pill called Levodopa, which is a medication used for Parkinson's disease at the time. I was to take the pill three times a day and, if the pill worked, we would notice a change within four days. He also wanted to see me one more time after I took the pills.

Once home, mom filled my prescription, and I was soon taking the pills, wondering if I would magically wake up straight the morning after I first took one. After one week, the pills had not made any change in my appearance and so I stopped taking them like the neurologist instructed.

We had a great family Christmas. There was the Christmas Eve service, reading the Christmas story on Christmas morning, eating fresh cinnamon rolls and drinking hot chocolate for breakfast, and then having the entire family over for dinner. Mom got free tickets to a Detroit Pistons game for each of us from her boss at work and all of us had a great time when we went a few days later. It was my first professional basketball game and were the players ever good looking!

During the holiday, the neurologist's office called and asked us to come back to Cleveland on January 7, 2008 to see a pediatric neurologist for his opinion and to then afterwards follow up with him. I was 18 at that time so I was right on the edge between being a pediatric and an adult patient

My parents and I drove back to Cleveland to see both neurologists. The pediatric neurologist checked my reflexes and took many pictures of me from different angles. He also took a video of me walking in different directions, and sitting, so that he could get the opinions of his colleagues as well. Then we went to see the adult neurologist and this time all we did was talk. He had consulted with the pediatric neurologist and both of them thought the next step should be Botox injections in the paraspinal muscles along my spine that were spasming. It seemed that if Botox didn't work, my case would be back in the orthopedic court.

It was hard to keep my eyes open on the way home since it was dark outside, and I was really full from our dinner. I will admit that I did close my eyes most of the way.

In preparation for the Botox treatments we went to one of the Toledo Clinics to see another neurologist and have another EMG done so he could determine what muscles Botox would be helpful to be injected in to. Sure enough, through all those needle pricks, he found a few muscles that were spasming, and he agreed that Botox might be beneficial for my paraspinal muscles. We set up an appointment to come back in ten days for the injections.

The next week we checked back with Dr. Munk about the neurologists' findings and he wrote a prescription for me to begin physical therapy sessions after the Botox was injected to ensure that we got the most benefit.

Then we were back the next day for the Botox injections but before he did the injections, the neurologist explained that Botox is a poison. I think he was trying to make sure I was fully aware of the risks before he went ahead. I told him I wanted to try it, since I really didn't have any other options, so he injected Botox on both sides of my spine. The shots were painless, though I had to remind myself to breathe! The whole process took no more than 15 minutes.

I started physical therapy the following week. The first week, I went three times, and then I had two sessions each week. At the end of each session, I laid on my stomach and a heating pad was placed over my back. It felt so good and helped me to relax.

**Excerpt from journal. *Heavenly Father, You have blessed my life very much. Knowing You makes me happy! I'm so glad that I am Yours! I long for everyone*

in this world to know You too, Father. I pray that You would use me, that I may show and teach others about Your love. Jesus, please give me the eyes to see, the ears to hear, and the words for me to say to those who may not know You. You are so beautiful, sweet Jesus! **

In May of 2007, it was decided that I should sell Farah. With all the surgeries I had, I was not able to ride her and I really wanted her to go to a home where she could be ridden on a regular basis. We found a great family but it was hard to see her go. Farah always seemed to sense when I was having a bad day and would let me hug, talk, and brush her for a long time. We made a great team!

10 Preoccupied

"Be joyful always; pray continually; give thanks in all
circumstances, for this is God's will for you in Christ Jesus."
1 Thessalonians 5:16-18 (NIV)

Our homecoming basketball game was in early February and it was a very good game even going into overtime. Typically, games were over by 9 pm but that night it was nearly 10 before it ended. I went to a friend's house to change and then, all dressed up, we went back to the school for the dance.

To begin with, the dance started late, and then we were informed that it had to be over by 11:30 because of a new state law that those under 17 are not to be driving past midnight. So let's just say it was a very short dance! We made the most with what little time we had!

The next week I had an appointment with Dr. Munk to check what effect the Botox treatment was having. When he examined me, he thought that the Botox treatments had calmed the spasming muscles but there was no effect on my overall appearance when standing. Dr. Munk mentioned surgery as a last resort and said he wanted us to see the orthopedic surgeon in St Louis again because if it came down to fusing the rest of my spine to the sacrum, he didn't feel comfortable doing it himself and would like Dr. Bridwell to possibly do it. He decided I needed to use the leg cuff again so we went back to the orthotic clinic and they reattached the cuff.

The following Monday there was a message on the answering machine from Helen, at Dr. Munk's office that they had scheduled an appointment in St Louis for me that very Friday if we could make it. That only gave us three days to get ready and find a hotel, but we were glad to have gotten in so soon.

We arrived in St Louis on Thursday evening, which was also Valentine's Day, and after checking in at our hotel, we decided to make a dry run to the hospital, just to make sure we knew the way. Later that evening dad and I worked out in the weight room, which felt good after sitting in the car for most of the day. I had trouble sleeping that night because I was very anxious about my upcoming appointment.

We were at the hospital just after 7am with my nerves on full blast. *"The Lord Himself goes before you and will be with you; He will never leave you nor forsake you. Do not be afraid; do not be discouraged." Deuteronomy 31:8 (NIV)* In my mind I kept repeating the phrase, *do not be afraid because God is going ahead of you and will be with you the entire time.*

The first step, after checking in, was to have new x-rays taken. Then we met with the orthopedic surgeon after he had studied them. In the x-ray I could clearly tell that my knee was bent because of how uneven my hips were. I have a habit of bending my knee with not even thinking about it. He said my back was worse than it was a year ago, but I had more of a pelvic obliquity (my pelvis was rotated and uneven), at this visit. He ordered three more x-rays so I headed back to the x-ray department. The first x-ray was on my legs. I had to lie on a measuring stick, and then a man took an x-ray of my pelvis, knees, and ankles. Then there was one taken of my spine when I was laying on my back, and then another one taken from a side view while also lying down. We never saw the surgeon after the x-rays were taken which was very frustrating because he didn't give us any guidance as to what else to do. I felt that if I ever had to have a spinal fusion surgery to the pelvis, I wasn't sure I would be comfortable having this surgeon perform it, even if he was one of the best. Bedside manner is also very important to me when picking a surgeon.

Through the many struggles and disappointments I found myself digging deeper into God's word and analyzing the meaning behind some of my favorite worship songs. My faith is what kept me going. I also had so many in our family and community lifting me up in prayer and offering me encouragement daily. People would also send me cards, which I really loved getting!

The following week I had an appointment with Dr. Munk. We had a lot of questions that day. Dr. Munk tried to answer our questions although I know he was just as frustrated because he wanted to get to the bottom of my case. He really didn't know what my future was going to hold and wanted me to see another orthopedic surgeon in Detroit for his opinion, and wanted a new MRI and CT scan done of my spine. He kept saying that doing more surgery was an absolute last resort. I think he wanted to wait to see if anything happened after the second round of Botox injections, as did I, which was scheduled at the end of April.

After my appointment, Mom and I went prom dress shopping. I wanted to find a dress I could wear without my brace, but I knew I would be uncomfortable the whole night if I didn't use my brace since I was really leaning. We were lucky because we found a beautiful dress at the first store that I could wear with my brace. When I walked out of the dressing room, all mom could say was, wow! The top of the dress was black and partway down it split and white lacy material stuck out. After looking at the dress on from all angles we decided this was the dress, I just needed my brace cut down a little and then the dress would be perfect. An older woman passed when I was admiring myself in the mirror and said that I looked like a darling doll. Not quite the reaction I was going for!

A week later we were headed back to Cleveland Clinic to see the pediatric neurologist. He reviewed the EMG and Botox report from my neurologist in Toledo and told us that there was no need for an EMG to be done on my arms and legs because that was not part of the problem. He was also disappointed at the amount of Botox I received. He said he would've injected my spinal muscles with ten times as much Botox as I was given; that way we would have known the results right away instead of doing a second round of injections. This information really blew us away. We were shocked that the doctors' views were so different.

I had to wait two more months before I could be injected again because our insurance only pays for Botox every three months, and since Botox is a poison, you have to be careful how far apart the injections are. So because we decided for convenience sake to have the injection done in Toledo instead of Cleveland, I was now three months behind in the treatment because of this decision.

**Excerpt from journal. *Each day, I need to live life, making it pleasing to God. I shouldn't worry about what happened yesterday, or what will happen tomorrow. I need to focus on today because today will soon be tomorrow and yesterday will be history. God will never give me more than I can handle each day, and so I need to give it all to the Lord because He is the only way I can make it through life's many trials. Today is the day, so let me live it!* **

The next evening I had my MRI and CT scan done at Toledo Hospital. The scans were scheduled at 6:30 and 7:00 pm so I didn't have to miss any school that day.

70

* * *

At the beginning of March my parents and I traveled to Detroit to consult another orthopedic surgeon at the Detroit Children's Hospital. The surgeon took a good look at me standing, sitting, and lying down on my stomach and back. He thought that it looked like something could be tethered inside my body because of how I was leaning. He also agreed that we needed to do the next round of Botox to determine what kind of results I would get the second time. He said that if the Botox works, it would not be a permanent fix but he wanted to wait and see.

He also suggested removing all of the hardware around my spine since I was nearly two years post-op from my first surgery. He said there could be a possibility of something in the hardware irritating me inside making me lean. He wanted to see my last MRI and CT scans just to be sure he didn't see something that others were missing.

From one of my last scans Dr. Munk did find that my L-5 level was tilted while lying down. This was not a prominent finding a year ago, but he still thought we should wait until the next Botox treatment before anything was decided, which I completely agreed with.

Over the past few months, I was having problems eating again so Dr. Munk thought I should have an upper GI series test done. I had an upper GI and small bowel series done at the Fulton County Health Center, which meant that, I had to drink a barium solution again, followed by a series of x-rays to track the solution in my GI tract. The results showed I had a very long, J shaped stomach and a low colon, which must not have been too concerning.

A few weeks later I had an appointment at the Westside Surgical and Pain Clinic in Toledo to find some relief for the lower back pain I was experiencing. The doctor said he wanted to try an injection in my lower back so we made an appointment in two weeks for the injection. This happened to be the night before my senior prom so I was hoping it wouldn't be too painful.

The following week I saw Dr. Munk again after he had a chance to talk with the surgeon I had seen weeks previously in Detroit. He mentioned that he would set up a tentative surgery date for the summer (2008) so that if the Botox didn't work he would take the hardware out. I was really hoping that this could be the problem, that I had an allergy to the instrumentation, which was causing my leaning, and that I would stand straight when it was removed.

"Now faith is being sure of what we hope for and certain of what we do not see."
Hebrews 10:19 (NIV)

When we were finished, Dr. Munk called the orthotic specialist and asked if he could trim my brace down if we headed over to his office. Since it was late, we hurried over to his office and waited as he worked his magic. A few days earlier, I had tried my prom dress on over my brace and then mom marked down where the brace needed to be trimmed at. He did an awesome job, and even trimmed it down a little lower so that way it'd fit under my dress perfectly and nobody would even be able to tell that I was wearing a brace. I left with a much lightened heart and was so grateful.

* * *

After many days of planning, April 11th, finally came. I was in charge of setting up a mock accident for our school before prom. It was the first time our school had ever done such a thing. A car was donated so it could be cut apart by the fire department. The accident was supposed to show the possible consequences of driving while intoxicated.

It was a beautiful day, a little chilly, but the rain had stopped and the fog had lifted. There were four victims, including me. While everyone was in first period class, we victims tore our clothes and put fake blood on ourselves. Then the fire captain came and positioned us in/on the car.

I was the DOA (dead on arrival) so my job was to lie on the hood of the car and look as if I had been thrown through the windshield. A tarp was placed over the car with only my feet sticking out. When the bell rang, grades 9-12 came out into the school parking lot with their chairs.

The show started with a 9-1-1 call followed by a second by second synopsis of what happens during an accident. The tarp was lifted off and everyone could see us. Sirens started coming from everywhere. I couldn't see much because I was the dead person and had to keep my eyes closed.

Soon a state patrol and a police car came to the scene, and then an ambulance, fire truck, and heavy rescue truck arrived. There sure were a lot of sirens going off! The police and an EMT took my pulse and then put a sheet over my head and pronounced me dead. Then the fire crew proceeded to use all their heavy duty tools to take off the roof of the car and the car doors. When Life Flight was getting ready to land, I thought I was going to blow right off the car because it was so windy!

After the three other passengers were taken away the hearse came and the funeral director and coroner came out and talked with the fire crew. Then everyone came over to me, and my heart began pounding really fast because I knew what would happen next. The fire crew, including my brother in law, Derek, took the sheet off me, and then told me they were going to roll me on my side and then put me on a back board. Then on the count of three, they lifted me onto a stretcher. It was then that they put me into a body bag and zipped it up, leaving my head out so I could breathe. Then I was wheeled into the back of the hearse. They locked me into place, shut the back door, left the parking lot, and then drove to the front of the school where they dropped me off. I couldn't get out until they took the straps off and unzipped the bag. Not many people can say they've been dropped off at school in a hearse.

I was so excited to do the mock accident, but after it was all done, it really hit me. It made me thankful that I was alive, and how drinking and driving is not worth it when you think of what can happen. It really seemed to be an eye opening experience for many of us, and afterwards everyone kept telling me how scary it was because I looked dead and I thought, that's the point!

I left school early that day because I had to wash off all the fake blood before my appointment in nearby Bowling Green with a gastroenterologist (GI). After examining me, he decided to put me on an appetite stimulate medication since I was often nauseous and losing weight. He also wanted me to have a gastric empty study test to see how well my stomach was emptying after I ate. A few days later I went to the Fulton County Health Center for the study. I ate some eggs with radioactive materials in them. I was supposed to eat as much as I could but I couldn't finish them. Then I laid down and a big scanner was placed above my abdomen. For ninety minutes, it monitored the radioactivity in my stomach. Since this study would take awhile, the tech put on Alvin and the Chipmunks for me to watch. Unfortunately the study ended before the movie so I didn't get to see the end of the movie, although my tech insisted I stay to finish it, but I had to get to school for an English test. This test showed that I had delayed gastric emptying.

The next day was my appointment to have the pain injections. The doctor gave me two shots to numb the area but the actual injection hurt more than I expected. I had to hurry back home afterwards because my prom date and I were going to go see a movie. I was just a little sore from the injections but not as bad as I thought I'd be.

* * *

It was finally the day of the prom. I ran two miles, did some homework, picked up my dates' corsage, and then went to get my hair done. Around 3pm I put on my makeup and my beautiful dress. Then my sisters and Derek came over to take pictures before my date arrived.

A brother-in-law's (Derek) Perspective

Your sisters came over to take pictures. I came over to be the protective "older brother" since you didn't have one. I was there to put fear in your date. Besides, I didn't get a chance to harass your date the year before, for your junior prom, because of the downtown fire I was helping to put out. FYI, I didn't let him in the door right away. And yes, you looked beautiful!

My date, Joe, was early. He drove up in a silver bug, and Derek answered the door. He looked great in his black tux with thin silver stripes and a silver and black vest. We put corsages on each other and then it was picture time. Then he led me outside to a silver Bug, opened my door, and I got in just as it began to sprinkle. We went to pick up my friend Rebekah and her date so we could all go together to the country club for dinner. That evening, while I was waiting in line for food, my high school principal came up and whispered in my ear that I looked very pretty, which made me grin from ear to ear. Since he'd had back surgeries also, he understood what I was going through. After dinner we drove back to school for the dance. The gym was decorated so well with dazzling lights across the ceiling and multicolored balloons covering the ground. It was fun, but I was so tired by the end of the night.

On May 3rd, I received my state FFA degree on the stage at the Ohio State FFA convention held in Columbus, Ohio. It was an awesome feeling walking across the stage in front of all those people, and it was quite an accomplishment. Being that I was the FFA reporter as well, I also received a State award for the chapter scrapbook that I put together over the past year.

In mid May, after waiting many months for the second round of Botox injections, we drove to the Cleveland Clinic. The pediatric neurologist explained again what he would be doing and the effects of Botox. He was going to inject ten times the amount of Botox that I had injected in Toledo, so they could determine if my condition was the result of an orthopedic or neurological problem.

He took an EMG along my paraspinal muscles so he knew which muscles to inject and then he injected the Botox. It didn't take very long and it wasn't too painful, just a few needle pricks. Then we drove home. After 24 hours there was still no change in my appearance so we were back in the orthopedic court.

That Friday night, our school hosted a Fellowship for Christian Athletes fun night where students involved in the Bible study at school came for a night of food, fun, and fellowship. I had been approached about the idea of sharing my testimony, and was a little hesitant at first because I get so nervous when speaking in front of a crowd. It didn't take me long to say yes though, because I knew that God would give me the words to speak. *"I can do everything through Him who gives me strength." Philippians 4:13 (NIV)* Once I started speaking, I felt myself relax. It was an honor to share my testimony with this group of students.

Once I got my prom dress for my senior prom, Dr. Munk had Dan from Cole Orthotics trim my brace down so that it would fit nicely under my prom dress. He did a fantastic job and no one would have ever known that I was wearing my brace under my dress. I could hardly eat anything for dinner though because of how tight I had to cinch my brace, but it was totally worth it!

11 Big Days!

But He said to me, "My grace is sufficient for you, for My power is made perfect in weakness." Therefore I will boast all the more gladly about my weaknesses, so that Christ's power may rest on me. That is why, for Christ's sake, I delight in weaknesses, in insults, in hardships, in persecutions, in difficulties. For when I am weak, then I am strong. 2 Corinthians 12:9-10 (NIV)

May 21, 2008 was the day I had been anticipating for a long time - my last day as a high school senior. All 49 of us arrived early that day and put balloons all over the high school and in some of the teachers' rooms. We also hung up crepe paper in the doorways and hallways. I'm glad I decided to get up early to help – it was so much fun!

When I went to work after school that evening I found out I had been randomly selected for a drug test when my shift was over. Me, of all people! I began to panic because I was taking narcotic pain medications at the time. I drank a lot of water that night at work and I called mom on my way to get tested because I was so nervous. She chuckled because she knew I'd fail the test, which really didn't make me feel any better. Well, I failed in over half the drugs that they tested me for, which was actually quite embarrassing. Luckily my boss knew my situation and told me not to think a thing of it. That was stressful!

My parents hosted a graduation party for me that Sunday and a lot more people came than we expected. Even Dr. Munk, Helen, Kitty, and all of their spouses came. (Dr. Munk even had an emergency surgery that morning but he still was able to come!) I was so excited to see them! While everyone was talking and munching, Dr. Munk and I had a chance to chat. It was so nice talking with him outside of the hospital and office setting where many times

I was often nervous. Everyone seemed to have a great time. And then when the party was over and everyone was gone we were all like vultures around the food table because we were hungry!

On Sunday, May 25th I received my high school diploma, and to my surprise, I also received a plaque for my high cumulative GPA, which made me so proud! Even with all the missed days over the years due to doctors' appointments and surgeries, I still managed to keep my grades up with the help and support of my teachers.

A few days later I had an EKG done at Toledo Hospital to check how the new medication I was taking to increase my appetite was affecting my heart. Afterwards I had an appointment with Dr. Munk. I weighed in at 100 pounds; I'd lost 8 ½ pounds in three months and I was one inch shorter than I was at my previous visit because of my lean. Botox had definitely had no effect on my posture.

He brought in a wrapped package and handed it to me, but we started talking so I set it to the side. He was trying to decide if he should take out both the rods and screws, leaving in markers where the screws were, or just take the rods and screws out from my lumbar , and not the thoracic, portions of my spine. After he examined me and took pictures, he left and his wife, Dorothy, poked her head in and told me to open the gifts. I could not believe it - they had gotten me a red digital camera, and a camera case! I was speechless! They knew I was going to Spain soon with my Spanish Club, and they wanted me to have a camera to capture my experiences. I had wanted a digital camera and had hoped to buy one before college, but I now had one and it was a great color!

Dr. Munk and Dorothy came back and asked if I liked it, and told me how difficult it was for them to decide on the color. Dorothy preferred pink and Dr. Munk liked black, so they compromised and got a red one. I was excited to try it out!

Dr. Munk had looked at my medical scrapbook at my graduation party and asked if I'd bring it in so he could take it with him to a medical conference. I brought it with us and gave it to him because I knew he'd take good care of it. I had such a thoughtful doctor and nurses!

As the days went by we got a phone call from Dr. Munk's office saying that surgery was postponed to July 22nd so I could have an endoscopy on July 1st, and have the results back before surgery. He also wanted to give me time to rest after my trip to Spain.

Spain was next on my schedule of events but in the days leading up to departure, I wasn't sure I should go. I really wanted to go, but I was in pain, which tired me. I didn't decide until the morning of departure but then it seemed to me I could either be in pain at home or in Spain, so I might as well go to Spain!

The next ten days in Spain were very tiring but so exciting. I had taken four years of Spanish in high school and went with several of my classmates and Spanish teacher. Each day was filled with many tours and exciting activities. The architecture and history of Spain was beautiful making me so glad that I had a new camera that worked great and took fantastic pictures! We visited six major cities in Spain, and traveled by train, subway, bus, boat, taxi and plane!

Many times we couldn't roll our luggage along because the streets were cobblestone. Two guys were assigned to help me and they lugged my luggage around with so much cheerfulness and good humor! I was very grateful!

I really wanted to find something special for Dr. Munk but I was having a rough time. Finally, I came across a little shop in Seville that made and painted such beautiful little clocks, and I immediately thought of Dr. Munk! My friend Rebekah and I went through the whole shop trying to find the perfect one - in the back of the store. We were almost left behind, but I had finally found the perfect gift! I came home exhausted - I'm sure everyone was – but I was so glad I went!

It was becoming hard to sleep through the night because of the pain in my back, both upper and lower so I resorted to taking cat naps throughout the day to keep my energy level up. Often at nights, if I was having a particular bad one, I would watch a movie after doing my devotions. My two older sisters had plenty of movies and kept me with a good supply. Watching a movie kept my mind temporarily off of the pain which is just what I needed, otherwise I would have spent the night staring at the ceiling and tossing and turning until finally my body would give into pure exhaustion.

On Sunday, June 22nd, my FFA teacher and some surrounding businesses put on a benefit for our family to help pay my medical bills. It was held in our school's gymnasium. Tables were set up and people helped themselves to BBQ pork sandwiches, baked beans, chips, coleslaw, and brownies. I couldn't believe all the people who came to help our family! There were many people I didn't know but this is so typical in our close knit community. It seems everyone had a good time and was well fed and they gave so generously. My family and I felt like a huge weight was lifted off our shoulders.

A week after the benefit, my parents and I received a very heartfelt letter from a man who played a big role in my life during high school. *"The manner in which Libbey has approached each decision along the way has been impressive. I will say that on many occasions when I knew Libbey was struggling with pain and medical issues, I struggled with her from an emotional standpoint. I didn't want her to ever have to deal with that-and wished I could have been able to do something about it. Being a mere mortal-I had to turn to prayer as my way of helping-and I will continue to do so."* This was only a portion of the letter, and when I read it tears came to my eyes. Although the past few years had been difficult, there had been so many blessings along the way. Whether those blessings were in the form of a hug, a prayer, a meal, a card, or a letter, I was being encouraged by so many, many of whom I never even knew.

* * *

On July 1st, we went to Toledo Hospital for my endoscopy. The procedure itself took only twenty minutes but it took me two hours to come out from sedation. The doctor showed some pictures of my stomach and esophagus to my parents and told them everything appeared normal. During the procedure he had taken some tissues for biopsy also, but that would take a few days until we got the results.

A week later I had an appointment at the University of Toledo Medical Center with a cardiologist because a few weeks earlier our family doctor wasn't able to find pulses in either ankle. Aside from my heart and circulation, the cardiologist checked the flexibility of my fingers, arms, and legs and found that I had an increased amount of collagen in my bones, which could be playing a part in my orthopedic problems. There is no cure for it or for the side effects of increased collagen. At the end of the appointment the doctor gave me a hug and a kiss. I had gotten many hugs from doctors but never a kiss from one!

Three days later, I received a package from the cardiologist in the mail. Inside was a book called, "When Bad Things Happen to Good People" by Harold S. Kushner. That was a really heartfelt gift as I knew that the doctor I had seen was a man of faith struggling in his own life with seeing someone he loved suffer. I was very appreciative of this gift and really enjoyed the book.

After that appointment, I saw Dr. Munk. When I took my brace and shoes off to be weighed and measured I was 5' 2" tall, quite a difference from my starting height of 5'6".

After my exam I had a chance to show my pictures of Spain to his friendly office staff while Dr. Munk finished with another patient. Then we sat down to talk and look at my x-rays. Initially it seemed as if he wanted to postpone the surgery again, but after much poking, prodding, and shifting my spine, and looking at the x-rays, he looked me in the eye and said, "The rods need to come out." Taking the rods out could eliminate the possibility of irritation from the rods, causing me to lean. He asked that we come back later in the week so his colleague could examine me. At this point I was officially on schedule for surgery on July 22nd at 8:30 a.m. At the end of the appointment I gave Dr. Munk the gift I had bought for him and Dorothy in Spain and he liked it!

We returned two days later to see his colleague. Dr. Munk came in with him and I was surprised to see Dr. Munk in shorts! (He was on his way to play golf.) His colleague watched me walk up and down without my brace five times so he could study a different part of me each time. After conferring with Dr. Munk he came back and told us he thought it was a good idea to take the rods out so if the leaning wasn't corrected after surgery, they knew that it was not due to the irritation of the rods. He also said that if the rod removal was not a success, then step two would be to do an osteotomy on the vertebrae in my lower back. This basically meant that they would chip some of the bone off of the lower vertebrae to help give my back the curve from front to back that it needed.

My back may have been hurting at that point because I didn't have the natural curve in my lower back. If that still wouldn't correct the leaning then step three would be to fuse the lower vertebrae to my sacrum, which would probably correct the leaning. I would have to wait four to six months between these surgeries because, when rods are taken out, there are often bone fragments still in the body, so they wait to give the body time to clean up the bone chips. He seemed very confident in our decision and in the possibilities of the future. We left feeling very confident and for me, I felt at peace with our decision.

The next morning, we got up very early so we could get back to Toledo Hospital for an MRI of my lumbar spine and pelvis. All the scans proved to be normal. I think Dr. Munk was hoping to see some irritation in the lower portion of my back so he would know that taking the rods out was the right thing to do.

On July 15, we were back for my pre-op appointment at the hospital and then mom and Grandma donated blood for me. The days leading up to my surgery went really fast. Some of my cousins were visiting and so I spent plenty of time over at my grandma's house.

Two nights before surgery, a couple in our church congregation organized a prayer meeting in our backyard. My family had thought it would be a small gathering, but it had been announced at the beginning of the church service, so that night, we were surprised by the turnout. Dad started the meeting by filling everyone in on the upcoming surgery, verses were read, and then we all gathered in a circle and sang a few worship songs, which sounded so beautiful. After singing, everyone broke into small groups to pray for a few minutes. It almost gave me shivers when I opened my eyes and looked at all the people lifting my doctors, family, and myself up in prayer.

Then everyone came back together in a large circle and discussed some of the things they prayed about specifically and spoke words of encouragement to us. When the prayer time was done, people came up and gave us hugs. It lasted about 1 ½ hours, and gave me a feeling of peace knowing that so many people were praying for me.

"What god is so great as our God? You are the God who performs miracles; You display Your power among the peoples." Psalm 77:13b-14 (NIV)

The next morning, I woke up with a bad stomach ache from nerves. Throughout the morning, I worked outside in the flower and vegetable gardens, which was one of my favorite places to be. Then I headed off to the library to get new books. It seemed as if the day was just flying by. That evening my friend, Rebekah, stopped by and we talked for over an hour. Afterward, I cleaned my room and packed a small bag for the hospital. As much as I was dreading surgery and being in the hospital again, I did hope I'd get a room in the new wing which opened only six months earlier!

**Excerpt from journal. *Sweet Jesus, I do love You so much. It is true, whether I am praying, singing, or reading of Your name, I feel more at peace and in Your presence. Mighty Father please let me feel Your embrace of comfort and love even more for I long to overflow my many blessings upon others for You are a great God, and I love You so much!* **

12 Surgery #4

"Do not be anxious about anything, but in everything, by prayer and petition, with thanksgiving, present your requests to God. And the peace of God, which transcends all understanding, will guard your hearts and your minds in Christ Jesus." Philippians 3:6-7 (NIV)

It was July 22nd, the morning of my fourth surgery. With my eyes still half shut, I hopped in the shower, and tried to really enjoy it! By 5:30 a.m. we were off.

Once I was prepped, Dr. Munk came in and greeted us. He explained what he planned to do and had me sign a few forms, because I was now 18. He checked my back and then went to change into scrubs. At 8 o'clock, my sisters and Derek came in for a quick visit. As my surgical nurse and Helen wheeled me back, we stopped at the kiss corner, as usual, where my whole family gave me hugs and kisses. I told them to not worry and that I'd see them soon! I was wheeled through many hallways until we stopped outside of my OR and I was slowly pushed into the hustle and bustle of my OR preparation. I was so cold and so my nurse piled warm blankets on top of me. After being attached to many monitors, the oxygen mask was held over my face, and not too long after I was out like a light.

A Sister's (Katie) Perspective

You would think watching you go back to surgery would get easier each time, almost like a routine. However, each time it gets worse and worse and worse. Whenever we reach the "kissing corner", I can't help thinking about how it's going to be for you when you wake up.

You're always the calm one among us in the pre-surgery room, always chipper and smiling! You even kept that smile on your face as they wheeled you down the hall towards your operating room. Every time they roll you away I just know that when you wake up you will just be in a horrible amount of pain. However, after each and every surgery, after a couple of days and all of your major surgery complications are over, you continue to have that smile on your face. I have no idea how you do it.

---

5 ½ hours later I was wheeled into the recovery room. Dr. Munk had taken some pictures of my spine when the rods were uncovered during surgery, and did find some inflammation at the base of my spine that did not show up in my MRI.

In the recovery room, I heard Dr. Munk tell my parents that they could come back to see me only if they promised not to wake me up because I needed my sleep. It seemed like I could always hear everything around me but yet I was sleeping too, which is kind of a strange feeling.

At 4:00 that afternoon, the recovery nurses decided it was time to wake me up. I remember how much pain I was in, feeling like my entire back was on fire. My nurse put a PCA (Patient-Controlled Analgesia) pump in my hand and told me to push the button when I needed medication, but I couldn't feel my hands or feet, which was rather scary. At the time I wasn't awake enough to tell them that. They kept telling me to push the button but I couldn't. I almost felt as if I was being punished, but I couldn't help it because I didn't have any feeling.

Later that evening I was wheeled to my room - in the new addition of the hospital! (Although I didn't know it at the time.) My family was there waiting for me. Finally I was able to tell someone that I couldn't push my PCA pump and so every six minutes my family would "help" me push it down.

The medicine felt wonderful and after a few pumps I began to feel much better. My heart rate had been really high and then it began dropping. Strangely enough, I could hear Annie counting down the numbers from my pulse oximeter monitor.

The alarms went off and a nurse came rushing in, listened to my heart, and began to massage my chest. She told me to breathe and take deep breaths, and yelled out for a nurse to get some oxygen. After I had oxygen, my heart rate and oxygen saturation levels returned to more normal levels.

Apparently the nurse paged Dr. Munk because he came in and listened to my heart also and checked my hands and feet because my family told him

I couldn't feel anything. He sent the pain medication to the lab to have it analyzed because I shouldn't have had that type of reaction. I couldn't have any more pain medication until my previous medicine was cleared out of my body. I went from having a small amount of pain medication every six minutes to nothing. My parents were on either side trying to comfort me but the pain was so intense and I kept crying. They gave me a shot of morphine but five minutes later the pain was horrible again, and after another shot of morphine with no relief, I was put back on my original pain medication. It took awhile but finally it took the edge off the pain.

I could always hear everything but I couldn't open me eyes because they were swollen from all the fluid and felt like lead.

The next morning Dr. Munk's resident came in, knelt down by the head of my bed, slightly shook me, and kept saying "Libbey, Libbey, can you open your eyes for me?" I was really wishing that I could!

Dr. Munk helped me sit up and eventually stood me up and helped me walk to a chair. It felt horrible, like all my skin was being pulled in every direction which I guess it probably was. I silently cried while I sat there. Dr. Munk held my neck up and wiped my tears away. After twenty minutes, I was helped back to bed. I was exhausted. I didn't think that this surgery was going to be nearly as painful as the others, but it was.

Throughout the morning and afternoon the nurses came in and helped me sit up. Dr. Munk's office staff came to visit me during their lunch hour, which was nice to have visitors.

By Friday morning I still wasn't fully awake. A neurologist stopped by to check me and he thought everything looked normal but he wanted a CT scan of my brain and an EEG (electroencephalogram) done just to be sure.

Dr. Munk sat me up in bed and helped me into my brace. After the brace was put on, his colleague came by and they tried to button my gown. They decided to race to see who could get finished first. It looked like his colleague finished first but then it was discovered that the buttons were uneven so he had to start over and so, in the end, Dr. Munk won. It made me chuckle knowing that these two great surgeons could repair complex orthopedic problems but couldn't figure out how the buttons went on a hospital gown! Afterwards they had me sit up and then stand.

A little while later, two transport staff came to pick me up and take me down to the CT lab. Next came the EEG where electrodes were placed on my scalp which would detect the electrical activity in my brain for forty-five minutes.

I finally woke up fully that afternoon, which meant the narcotics finally got flushed out of my body. This was good timing because my pastor and grandparents came to visit that afternoon, so I was able to sit and talk with them. I finally went for a short walk too. I was a little wobbly, but it was nice to see what life looked like from outside of my hospital room.

Later on Derek and Katie came and they ended up staying fairly late. (That was partly because Derek was really enjoying the huge cable TV.)

The next morning, which was also Dr. Munk's birthday, I was discharged. We got him a frame that said: **Faith** *makes things possible not easy;* and a huge bag of jolly ranchers because we had found out they were his favorite candy! He gave me a few prescriptions and then gave me a hug and a kiss and then left to compete in a dragon boat competition in downtown Toledo. I understand his team ended up doing very well. The ride home was very bumpy and again quite painful.

When I got home, my family and Lenney were so excited to see me. It was very nice to be home!

As the days passed, I was determined not to just sit and wait to feel better. I was up and walking laps around our house every morning and evening to try to gain my strength back and to get rid of the surgical pain and bloating.

Excerpt from my spiritual journal. *Sweet Jesus, what a glorious day that will be when we stand in Your presence and all the pain and pressures of this earthly life will be wiped away, and every minute, every hour, and every day of each year will be spent worshipping You with everything that is within me for You deserve all the glory and honor. You are an awesome God full of love, who hates to see any of His children crying, in pain, or afraid. I love You so much and I wait for that day in eager anticipation when the burdens of this world will be no more and I'll see You, Jesus, face to face!*

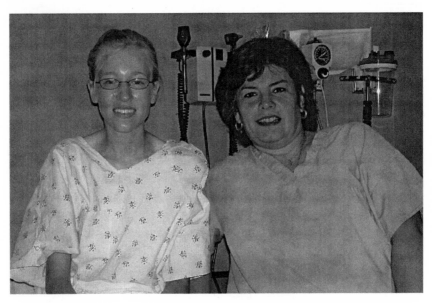

Before each of my surgeries, Helen, who is Dr. Munk's nurse, helped wheel me back to the OR and stayed with me until I was put to sleep. Having her there was always reassuring and helped me to relax!

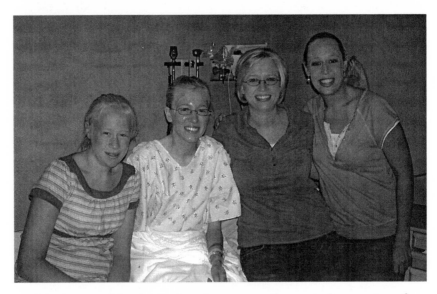

My sisters and brother in law always came down on the morning of my surgeries. I was so glad that they were able to take off work because I really liked my whole family to be there. We were all nervous and tired but we always have a way of having fun when we are all together! Pictured above from left is Annie, me, Katie, and Rebekah.

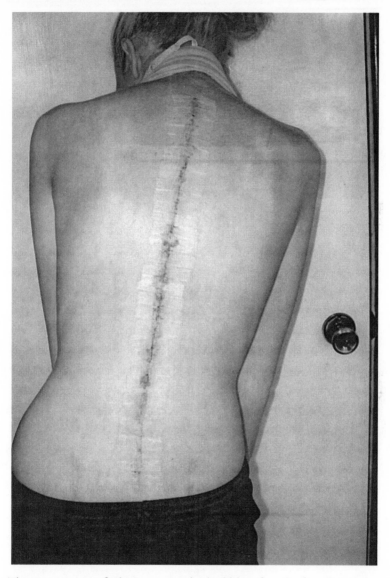

This is a picture of what my spine looked like after the fourth surgery. Had we known that I was going to need more than one surgery, it would have been much easier if Dr. Munk would have just put a zipper in my back after the first one!

13 Shrinking...Again

"Who shall separate us from the love of Christ? Shall trouble or hardship or persecution or famine or nakedness or danger or sword? Romans 8: 35 (NIV)

Ten days later I had an appointment with Dr. Munk. While waiting, Dorothy gave me my scrapbook back that Dr. Munk had taken to a medical conference. In the back page he had put three pictures that were taken during surgery when my back was opened up with the rods and screws still in. These pictures were quite fascinating.

After Dr. Munk came in, I stood up and walked down the hallway a few times for him without my brace on. He massaged my back to relax the muscles and then sent me for x-rays. While waiting for my x-rays, some of the office ladies came back in the room to say hello. Everyone was so nice, so I am not sure why I got so nervous for appointments.

The x-rays didn't look quite as good to Dr. Munk as he had hoped but he said he was guardedly optimistic of the outcome. He thought we should be able to tell if the surgery helped or not within a few weeks. Because I was still having gastrointestinal problems he recommended that I see a GI specialist in Columbus, Ohio.

I had been accepted into the nursing program at Indiana Wesleyan University (Marion, Indiana) that fall but I wasn't feeling well, I was still leaning, I had no appetite, and very little energy. I also knew that I would still have many doctors' appointments over the next few weeks and months. All of these factors helped me to decide to attend a nearby community college, which would also enable me to work part time at the nursing home. It was hard to be put on a long waiting list for the nursing program at the community college, after being accepted into the IWU nursing program, but I felt that I had made the right decision.

After six weeks without seeing any changes in my posture, we went back on September 17 for an appointment with Dr. Munk. My posture was slightly worse than it had been at my previous appointment which was disappointing for everyone. He massaged my back for a long time, trying to get my spinal muscles to relax, and had me lie down in different positions. Then he called in his colleague to examine me as well. Both doctors felt that I had a neurological problem, not an orthopedic problem, even though I had seen several neurologists who felt that I had an orthopedic problem and not a neurological one, which was frustrating. Dr. Munk recommended that I should have another MRI of my entire thoracic and lumbar spine to make sure everything was okay from that perspective. I realized it was still early on in the healing process, but I just wanted to stand straight again and would do and try anything.

**Excerpt from journal. *Hope is one thing that we can hold on to. When it seems that nothing is going right, we can always have hope in Jesus for He will pull us through, and do great things in our lives. I love You, Jesus, and thank You so much for giving us hope in such a dark and sinful world, for we can make a difference and make it brighter through your love, grace, and kindness!* **

A few days later I meet with the pain management specialist again. He said before he tries more injections he would like to have me fitted with a TENS (Transcutaneous Electrical Nerve Stimulation) unit. Electrode patches would be put on my back and hooked to a machine called a TENS unit that sends nerve impulses into the muscles to alleviate the pain. In a few days we were going to meet with a representative who could fit me with one.

That afternoon we headed over to Toledo Hospital for my MRI but they were running 1 ½ hours behind. While waiting we went to the hospital cafeteria, which has great food, for supper, and then walked in the park across from the hospital. It was a beautiful evening and it felt great to get out and walk.

The MRI took 1 ½ hours and it seemed much longer because I had no music. Halfway through the scans, one of my earplugs fell out. I didn't want to move and mess up my scans so I didn't even try to put it back in. When it was all over I couldn't hear very well out of that ear for quite awhile.

Two days later, my parents and I traveled to Columbus to see a gastroenterologist at the Nationwide Children's Hospital. Every year our FFA donated money to the hospital so it was neat to actually see it.

While we waited for my appointment we took a walk. Suddenly we heard my name called over the hospital loudspeaker to report back to the G.I. waiting room. We were surprised and hurried back to find that the doctor had a cancellation ahead of me and he could see me sooner.

He was a very nice doctor with an Italian accent. After the examination, he concluded that my stomach problem was very likely due to my back problems and surgeries. He prescribed two new medications to see if that would speed up my stomach motility. We were to return to see him in two months, and by then the new GI clinic would be finished.

The next day, we went back to Toledo to have me fitted for my TENS unit. When the technician was explaining everything it seemed overwhelming but when I sat down that evening and read the instructions it made sense after all. It had been a week of running all over the countryside for appointments and we were ready to just stay home!

In mid-October I had an appointment with a neurologist in Toledo. He talked with us about some rare neurological diseases that he wanted me to be tested for. I was really hoping I didn't have any of them. He started me on a new medication for muscle spasms and ordered a lot of blood work. Luckily, all the tests came back within normal limits.

During the month of October, I had the chance to shadow my neighbor, who is a doctor, two days a week in the Emergency Room at our local hospital. Some days the ER was really busy and other days he had time to sit down and explain what he looked for on radiographs. I got to interact with patients of all ages. It was very nice to be on the other side of the bed and being the one giving encouraging smiles, rather than being the patient.

One day at college when I had a little time to spare before my next class, I began creating a blog called Straighten the Path for Scoliosis. I wrote about my thoughts and what happened at my doctor's appointments. It was fun to create and I really enjoyed writing on it.

At the beginning of November I had an appointment with Dr. Munk. It was in the late afternoon so I came home a bit early from school and took our dog, Lenney, out for a walk in the woods behind our house. When we reached a clearing, three deer ran across the field right in front of us. I almost had a heart attack! When we were coming back through the woods, two more deer were startled by our presence and jumped out of their hiding place. I couldn't believe our luck!

When we got to Dr. Munk's office, I was weighed and measured. The tallest I had ever been without my brace was 5'6" back in 2005. Now I was 5'4" in the brace and 5'0" without it. This means I was really leaning to my right. Before my third surgery, my spinal alignment was 20 centimeters off from my cervical spine to my lumbar spine and now after the fourth surgery my alignment was 25 centimeters off. This was all really discouraging.

Dr. Munk had me stand up and lay on my stomach, back, and both sides while he analyzed and massaged my back muscles. He didn't really know what to do next or where to send me. He looked at some of my old x-rays while I asked questions and told him what I was experiencing and mom did too. He gave us two doctors' names that he thought I could see.

That appointment left me feeling a little frustrated because I didn't want to be crooked, in pain, and utterly exhausted for the rest of my life. I also felt for Dr. Munk because I knew he really wanted to figure out my case but it seemed like we were running into dead ends. "You Are Everything" by Matthew West came on the radio on our way home and gave me some strength when I really needed it. *"You are everything that I live for. Everything that I can't believe is happening; you're standing right in front of me with arms wide open. All I know is every day is filled with hope because you are everything that I believe for. And I can't help but breathe you in, breath again, feeling for this life within every single beat of my heart."* I was feeling sad and discouraged, but after hearing this song I had to think that every day is filled with hope, but it is up to me to have an attitude that anticipates and reflects that.

As my family and I considered how things were, we all thought we should see the orthopedic surgeon in St. Louis again because he was an expert on fusing down to the sacrum, and that could be my next step. So Mom called his office the next day and we were scheduled for an appointment in only three weeks.

In mid November I saw the gastroenterologist again to review the medications I was taking to increase my appetite. Because I hadn't gained any weight or had any other immediate results, he doubled my doses to see if that would help. He kept emphasizing that we needed to get the back problem figured out because it was more than likely causing the stomach problems.

**Excerpt from my journal. *Sweet Jesus, You are awesome and I love You with everything that is within me! Jesus, physically I have not been healed, but through this difficult journey, You have healed me spiritually! This is so great because without hope and faith in You, I don't know how I'd get through the physical* *difficulties. Jesus, my hands are reaching out to You. My faith in You helps to control the physical pain that I experience. I love You so much and I pray that You will continue to mend and strengthen my heart for You.* **

* * *

The days leading up to my appointment with the orthopedic surgeon in St Louis couldn't seem to go fast enough, and it was all I could think about. I was excited that he might be able to try to fix my spine, but I was very nervous that he would say there was nothing he could do to help and he made me a bit uncomfortable. I was trying not to get my hopes up too much.

The weather was awful as we set out for St Louis. The roads were covered with snow and ice making them very slippery. It took a little over eight hours before we finally saw the big St. Louis arch in the distance.

That evening we ate at a delicious root beer factory and after returning back to our hotel that evening, dad and I went into the exercise room. Dad certainly made me laugh when he commented how he could feel his stomach bouncing up and down while running on the treadmill, which was no surprise considering the size of the hamburger he had eaten for supper!

When we arrived at the massive hospital complex the next afternoon, the waiting room was very full and we heard that several patients had been waiting a few hours. We knew we were in for a long wait.

Because I had had surgery since my last visit, I had to go have updated x-rays taken. After that the surgeon analyzed my movement and appearance from all angles. He told us that he did not feel that I should be fused down to my sacrum yet because he wanted to have "every stone unturned" first. We had seen so many doctors, over twenty different ones at this point, and I had had so many tests done that I thought that most "stones" had been unturned. He wanted me to be put under general anesthesia again to see if I would straighten out when I was in a totally relaxed state, which could determine if my spine was still fixable.

We went home with very heavy hearts, because we had hoped this surgeon would have had something more encouraging to say. On the way home, we had a Christian radio station on and the verse of the day came from Revelation 21:3b-4 (NIV) *"Now the dwelling of God is with men, and He will live with them. They will be His people, and God Himself will be with them and be their God. He will wipe every tear from their eyes. There will be no more death or mourning or crying or pain.* Tears glistened in my eyes as I heard this verse. It was a reminder to me that Jesus also suffered when coming to this earth, so He knew exactly what I was going through even though it seemed as if no one else did. I couldn't wait for that day when there'd be no more tears, pain, or fears in this life. When we got home there was a message on our answering machine saying that I had an appointment to see a pain specialist at the Cleveland Clinic that Friday. It was very unexpected, but that raised the hope that maybe another door would be opened.

That night in my devotions, I came across a beautiful prayer that summed up just how I was feeling. *"Lord, sometimes life is difficult. Sometimes, I am worried, weary, or heartbroken. But, when I lift my eyes to You, Father, You strengthen me. When I am weak, You lift me up. Today, I turn to You, Lord, for my strength, for my hope, and my salvation. Amen"* I knew that in God's timing He would heal me the way He saw fit to, it was finding that hope when I was faced with discouraging days and doctor's appointments.

A Father's Perspective

Looking over the past few years, I've seen how much my faith in God has grown. As a father you try to keep your children protected and out of harm's way. You don't want to see them in pain. Sometimes I've learned we have no control. Watching Libbey's back twist and turn with no explanation from anyone, why? What do we do next? Why is this happening to her? How can I help her?

On Friday we went to the Center for Spine Health at the Cleveland Clinic. We were a little early so for fun, we took the elevator up the fifteen stories, stopping at each floor on the way down and hoping no one wanted on with us! The pain management specialist didn't need to examine me long before he concluded that I should be seen by an orthopedic surgeon. He referred me to one of his colleagues at the clinic, after calling him for his opinion. We were to come back the following Wednesday for the appointment; and beforehand, the surgeon wanted a CT scan of the thoracic/lumbar portion of my spine. We were relieved to get an appointment so soon, but I was stressed because that would mean I would miss my one exam at college.

That night I got to work on my take home exam and my last paper so they'd be ready to turn in on the Monday before my appointment. Luckily all went well, so well that I got a 4.0 GPA that semester!

On December 10 we headed back to Cleveland. I had the CT scan of my thoracic and lumbar spine early on in the morning at the clinic. After changing into a gown, I was so embarrassed walking through the crowded waiting room and hallway without my brace on because of how crooked I was. I felt as if all eyes were on me, even though they probably weren't. After my scan, we walked around the Cleveland Clinic and admired all the Christmas decorations, and later on it was time for us to go meet with the orthopedic surgeon.

The doctor had me stand up and walk, and then lay down and sit up. He didn't have to examine me long before he was pretty sure he knew the problem. He said that I was definitely a surgical fix. He said that my CT scan showed there was a possible fracture at the T 10/11 level of my fusion. Then he just seemed to fit the puzzle pieces together. Everything made so much sense and it seemed to all fit together perfectly. We were very impressed that he came up with a diagnosis without reading the notes from the other surgeon's opinions. He answered many of our questions without us even needing to ask. He said he wanted to look at the latest CT scan and all my x-rays in more detail but, overall, he felt that my back needed to be broken, realigned, instrumentation put back in, and then have an osteotomy to reposition the bone and give me a natural curve. This was quite a drastic measure that he was proposing to correct my spine and we left with much to think about.

My parents really wanted a second opinion. My mom had read an article in a recent magazine about a surgeon who was performing complex spine surgeries in Africa and after doing some online research she came across world class spine surgeon, Dr. Oheneba Boachie-Adjei. He voluntarily does complex spine surgeries in Africa through an organization that he created called FOCOS, but also has an office in Manhattan, NYC.

My parents thought it would be good to get his opinion, if possible. I wasn't thrilled about it because I had just had a doctor say he could fix me and I didn't want to see somebody else who might say there was nothing to be done. And I was just tired of seeing doctors in general, and I certainly didn't want to go to New York City. We live in the country surrounded by cornfields, so NYC would be quite different and I didn't think I'd like being in such a big city. But a few days later, mom called and got an appointment that was only five weeks away, on January 26, 2009.

**Excerpt from journal. *Knowing You Jesus, is the best thing that can ever happen to a person. Life is full of twists and turns Jesus, and doesn't always go our way. Life can be very difficult but Jesus, You can move the mountains that are towering in our lives. These mountains that we experience mold us into the people we are today, and can make us even better people because of them. I love You Jesus, and I am so grateful that You gave up Your life for me. My heart swells with love and gratitude for You!* **

We waited to hear back from the orthopedic surgeon at Cleveland Clinic but they didn't return our messages. Finally the surgeon's secretary called and said the surgeon wanted to see me again after we returned from New York City, and I began to have a few doubts about him.

On Tuesday, December 30, we went to the Toledo Hospital. I was scheduled to have an MRI at 7:00 a.m., but we were told that I needed to be there at 6:30 to register. After the MRI, I was going to be put under general anesthesia to see if my spine straightened out. We were a little bit early and so we walked around the hospital, which was really quiet that early. In the new lobby of the hospital they had a 25 foot Christmas tree that was loaded with decorations, and was quite a site.

Once in the MRI waiting room I had to fill out a questionnaire and change into a gown. I just found out when my tech was going through my paperwork that the MRI was of my head, cervical, thoracic, and lumbar spine which would take approximately two hours.

It was a long time to lie still, and I was very uncomfortable lying on my back and so I couldn't help but move around a little. A few scans had to be re-done because you are not supposed to move, although I didn't think I moved that much.

At 8:45, I was finally able to sit up and have a short break which felt wonderful and was really needed. My tech injected me with contrast for clearer scans and then it was back in the tube for more scans. By the time I was finished it was nearly 9:30. We hurried to the surgical waiting room, which was very busy.

I was taken back to a pre-op room where right away, my anesthesiologist came in to ask some questions before I even had a gown on. Dr. Munk came in and examined me, and when he walked outside my room to fill out some paperwork, my nurse came back and put an IV in. We were under pressure but she found a vein on the first try, which was exciting because that rarely happened!

When she was done, my surgical nurse, named Anne, came to get me, but the pre-op nurses weren't quite ready for me to go yet and were scrambling around finishing some last minute paperwork. She put a cap on my head while we waited and then we were off to the OR casting room where I was greeted by Dr. Munk and my anesthesiologist. I was wheeled in and had to roll unto the bed they had for me.

They were having problems because first there were no straps on the table to hold me in place and so they had to go find some. Then there were no arm rests attached to the table, so they had to find those too. Then it was just Dr. Munk and me in the room. He was trying to find the button to put the head of the bed up so that it would be more comfortable for me while we were waiting. Instead, he kept moving my feet up and down and then the head down instead of up. It was rather amusing, and we never did find out how to put the head up because others came back into the room so it was time to get started!

The nurse anesthesiologist came in, put leads on my chest, and then gave me the relaxant injection. The last thing I remember is when they put the oxygen mask by my face, I could not stop coughing, which was rather annoying and had never happened before when I was put under anesthesia.

Dr. Munk then moved and shifted my spine and took x-rays while I was under because my muscles were all completely relaxed and he was able to determine if he could still achieve some correction.

My x-rays taken showed that my spine straightened out when under general anesthesia which was great, because they knew that I was still fixable! I went in to the recovery room at 11:45 a.m. and woke up an hour later with a migraine. I was given three injections of a pain medication, which relaxed me but didn't do much for pain and so my nurse gave me two injections of morphine, which was wonderful and probably too strong because I slept all afternoon.

Finally, at 5:00 p.m., I was awakened, so that I could go home. It was rough because I wanted to keep sleeping! I was very grateful to pop in a few Tylenol, hug Lenney, and hit the couch when we got home, and was I ever ready to go to bed later that night!

On January 16th, 2009, we left for the Nationwide Children's Hospital in Columbus to see my gastroenterologist. When we got to the GI clinic, I was weighed and measured. I had lost two pounds again but was still 5' 4" in my brace which was good because I didn't shrink any more. My doctor wanted to put me on two new medications, although the one was used mainly in Germany, so could be difficult to get our hands on. He really emphasized again that we needed to get the back problem figured out first. It was a good visit but made for a long day.

On January 19th, mom and I drove to Toledo to see my neurologist, because the MRI that I had done in December showed some slight demyelinization of my right cerebellum, which is in the brain. Demyelinization means that there is a loss of myelin, which insulates nerve endings and helps them to receive and interpret messages at a high speed from the brain. Dr. Munk had reassured us that it was probably nothing but felt that should be seen by a neurologist just to be sure.

We were told that heavy "jolts," such as me being bucked off my horse, can cause some demyelinization in the brain, so that is more than likely what they saw. Multiple Sclerosis (MS) can also show these types of spots in the brain, so that is what the doctors were slightly concerned with me having, but I did not have any other symptoms of MS. Apparently I also had those spots in my brain two years previously when I had a brain MRI done, but they were very slight, and were not significant then.

They wanted me to have another brain MRI in one year just to make sure. After the appointment, we went to the Family Christian Bookstore and I finally got to get a new Bible. In the past two and a half years, I had read through the Bible twice and I was ready for a new Bible. Since some nights I was not able to fall asleep due to lower back pain I read the Bible and watched movies on my laptop.

**Excerpt from my journal. *Jesus, while everything may seem to be crumbling around us, You are the one thing that stands firm always, which is so comforting. You are always beside me through this journey of life here on earth. I need to trust all the time that this is Your plan for my life, and that You won't ever leave me standing on my own. You will lift me up and hold me in Your arms when it seems that the load is too heavy for me to carry. You are the ultimate way.* **

14 Renewed Hope

"And we rejoice in the hope of the glory of God. Not only so, but we also rejoice in our sufferings, because we know that suffering produces perseverance; perseverance, character; and character, hope. And hope does not disappoint us, because God has poured out His love into our hearts by the Holy Spirit, whom he has given us."
Romans 5:2b-5 (NIV)

On January 24, 2009, my parents and I took a flight from the Detroit Airport for New York City. I was still dreading the trip because of the doctor appointment that awaited me. I didn't want to get too disappointed if the doctor said he couldn't do anything to help me. I closed my eyes and rested for most of the flight but I was fully awake when we flew over the Statue of Liberty and Manhattan. I couldn't help but get a little excited about visiting NYC after seeing that!

We didn't do much that evening other than getting settled in at our hotel. We took a walk but it was very cold and we were tired from our trip.

The next day we started by finding the subway station and then we bought metro cards (which was rather confusing to us country folks and didn't amuse the people behind us!). Our first destination was Ground Zero and the 9/11 museum nearby. We also visited St. Paul's Chapel where many rescuers slept and ate. Then we walked along the Hudson River for a while and went inside the World Financial Center to warm up a bit. Finally, we took the subway down to Battery Park to see the Statue of Liberty, but it was so cold and windy by the river and it was getting dark so we headed back to Times Square. What an awesome and magical place it was with all the flashing lights!

We just couldn't pass the massive M&M store in Times Square without stopping in. With all the varieties and colors of M&M's, we decided we had to try some. We filled up a small bag and then mom went to pay. Was she ever surprised when she saw the price! The M&M's were nearly fifteen dollars per pound! We knew right then we weren't in Northwest Ohio anymore.

The next morning, Monday, we hailed a taxi to take us to my appointment with Dr. Boachie-Adjei. Once checked in, I had a packet of paperwork to fill out and then we waited for hours. The nurses were very kind which helped me become a little less nervous. They had me change into a gown and gave me a pair of very large green shorts to put on. I felt so self-conscious walking in the hallways without my brace on, and really began hoping that this doctor may have an answer or solution to help me stand straight again.

Dr. Boachie's fellow (meaning he/she is a physician who enters a medical specialty after completing his/her residency) first came in and had the fun job of sorting through all my x-rays. He examined me, asked a lot of questions and then went out to look at the CD's of x-rays, MRI's, and CT scans of my spine. We could hear him talking with Dr. Boachie outside my door but we couldn't hear what they were saying.

Dr. Boachie and his fellow then came back in and he introduced himself. He seemed to be a very compassionate doctor. He examined me and then looked at the x-rays we brought. He wanted some pictures of my posture, so everyone left and a nurse came in. She had me put on a bikini-like top and then a black background was rolled down behind me. She took pictures from just about every angle. Then I was sent to have more x-rays taken. Dr. Boachie was there to help position me to get the best x-ray view possible.

While I was waiting in the room for the x-rays to develop, the x-ray tech motioned for me to come over to his computer. He pointed out what he was doing to ensure the best views were showing. It was fascinating and I even got a sneak peak of what my x-rays looked like before anyone else.

My newest x-rays were hung up in my exam room and then Dr. Boachie and his fellow came back in to look at the latest x-rays, which were the clearest ones I'd ever seen. The room was quiet and I was holding my breath in anticipation of what he'd have to say. After analyzing them and taking measurements, he finally broke the silence and told us he thought I should be fused to the sacrum. I felt a weight lifted off of my shoulders.

He said there was a lot of stress on my lower spine which would eventually break down if nothing was done. By fusing my spine to the sacrum he could correct the leaning, though there was a chance I might still lean forward. The fact that I didn't lean forward when I was in the brace was a good indication that I might stand straight afterwards. In addition, he felt physical therapy would strengthen my muscles in the weeks following the surgery. We asked Dr. Boachie his opinion about the surgeon's suggestion we had seen that said my back should be broken and realigned, but Dr. Boachie was strongly against that. We were very pleased with Dr. Boachie, and my feelings of dread turned into feelings of hope.

After our appointment, we met with a staff nurse to discuss the overwhelming cost of surgery because Dr. Boachie was not in our insurance network. We felt comfortable with him and with his decision and I felt he was the right doctor to perform this next needed surgery. I really respected his dedication to taking mission teams from the Hospital for Special Surgery to Ghana to perform life changing surgeries. With our decision made, his nurse told us they would call us within a week with a possible surgery date. The next afternoon we flew home and waited to hear from them regarding the date and for surgery codes so we could get some information from the insurance company to see how much they would cover, if any.

The following week we saw Dr. Munk. I was worried that he might not agree with Dr. Boachie's decision. I highly respect Dr. Munk and his opinions of my care. Dr Munk said he thought very highly of Dr. Boachie and had worked with him in a few orthopedic workshops and he would do any pre-op/post-op testing and care because New York City was quite a trip. That was what I wanted to hear, that we were all in this decision together. I left the appointment feeling as if a weight had been lifted from my shoulders, and also felt that I had received Dr. Munk's blessing to go ahead with surgery.

How many people can say they are excited to have surgery? I knew it was going to be very painful, but I was full of hope that I would stand up straight again without wearing a brace. *"And my God will meet all your needs according to His glorious riches in Christ Jesus." Philippians 4:19 (NIV)* There are so many times that I have to remind myself that God will meet my needs in His timing as long as I fully rely on Him.

When we got home my parents told Annie she could come with us to NYC, so she was just about as excited as I was because it meant so much to have my family with me before surgery. We were all happy that we had found another confident, skilled surgeon that we felt comfortable with, and my sisters and grandparents also supported our decision. *"And we know that in all things God works for the good of those who love Him, who have been called according to His purpose." Romans 8:28 (NIV)*

A few days later we got a call from Dr Boachie's office that my surgery was set for June 17th at the Hospital for Special Surgery with Dr. Boachie. We would have to leave for NYC a week ahead of my surgery because there were many pre-op testing and appointments with various doctors. This would also give us some time for sightseeing.

This gave me a period of 2 ½ months when I had no doctor's appointments. I could work and go to school without having to switch my schedule around, but I knew it was just the calm before the storm!

We had a lot to do. We received the surgery codes in the mail so dad checked with our insurance company in hope that they would cover a small part of the total cost. (His blood pressure seemed to rise every time he called them.)

We also had to find a rental apartment in the city. This was difficult because we weren't sure how long we would need to stay in the city after surgery and everything depended on how mobile I would be afterward. Dr. Boachie said that I might be put into a cast that extended to my right knee.

My job was to track airline ticket prices online. As soon as we saw a small drop in the prices we bought four. My parents also found and booked a rental apartment for five weeks. The apartment was on the 21st floor. This would be quite a change for all of us, as we live in the country surrounded by cornfields.

Meanwhile, I was going to school part time at a nearby community college, working as a dietary aide in a nursing home, and cooking for my family at home.

At the end of April mom and I went to Flower Hospital in Toledo for pre-surgical testing. My whole afternoon was filled with tests. I had an echocardiogram, complete pulmonary testing, and a bone density scan.

**Excerpt from journal. *Jesus, I am always desperate for Your loving arms. Life would be nothing without You. Jesus, Your love, amazing love, is always enough; enough to make it through the day and through the many trials and burdens in life. I love You so much. I always need You. I know that You know exactly how I feel and You are always next to me whispering encouragement in my ear when I need it, and You are there to carry my burdens when they become so heavy that it is impossible for me to carry alone. You give me life, and I love You with all my heart!* **

* * *

On May 3rd, Smith's Restaurant helped to host a benefit at my church for my medical expenses. My mom works as a hostess at Smith's, and didn't find out that they were putting on a benefit until a few weeks before because they wanted to surprise her. The restaurant provided a delicious main entrée while my church provided the tasty desserts. This was the second benefit for my family within a year's time which was very humbling. It was an answer to prayer because, as much as I wanted to have the surgery, the cost was immense.

I set up a table with pictures from previous surgeries and provided cards for people to write notes of encouragement on for me. After the benefit, I tucked them away to read while I was recovering. So many people came to encourage us and it meant so much to have their support. Even Dr. Munk and his wife came, which meant more to me than I can say, and my grandparents were able to meet them. Everyone had a great time and we had plenty of leftovers to take home.

Two weeks later I had the honor of talking with the second graders at Pettisville Elementary School about my scoliosis journey up to that point. They were very intuitive and asked many great questions. I was even able to take in three x-rays to show, which helped them to understand what scoliosis looked like. I also made little bone sugar cookies to pass out on their way back to class, which they absolutely loved. Each year the second graders put on a consumer fair in the gymnasium where they make a project to sell and they donate the money earned to someone or someplace in need. That year the money was donated to my family for medical expenses and it was greatly appreciated!

With all the surgeries I had and the constant pain, shaving my legs was quite difficult, so I didn't do it very often. While shopping one afternoon, I found a leg wax kit that could be done at home. It sounded like such a great idea and I couldn't wait to try it out. Later that evening, mom tried it on my legs, which was much more difficult than the directions stated. Instead of the wax pulling off as it's supposed to, half of it came off and half of it stayed on my legs. Needless to say we stopped before the job was done because we were making a sticky mess. Lenney came up to investigate and his ear got stuck to my leg. So then he put his paw up to get his ear unstuck and his paw got stuck too. It was quite funny and mom and I were laughing so hard. We couldn't find anything to take the wax off, but luckily dad had a solution. He brought home some of the special soap he uses in the shop that gets everything off and, sure enough, it took the wax off. I learned my lesson, and won't try that again.

On May 27th I went to Toledo to have a CT scan of my pelvis so Dr. Boachie could see where to place the screws in my pelvis during my upcoming surgery. This was necessary because I'd had two bone grafts taken from both sides of my pelvis already. I had to drink a large bottle of thick liquid contrast called Ready Cat, because it helps to get more precise images.

After the scan, I had an appointment with Dr. Munk. Without my brace on I had shrunk another inch. I was 5'1" with my brace off and around 5'4" with it on. Before I had scoliosis, I was 5'6". I was hoping I would gain my height back with this next surgery. I got so many hugs and words of encouragement from his office staff that I wished I could pack them up and take them with me to NYC. One of them even came to Smith's Restaurant for breakfast a few days later and gave mom a pair of pajamas for me and a gift card for my favorite store, the Family Christian Book Store. That meant so much to me!

The next day I had an afternoon appointment with my neurologist in Toledo. He talked with us for a while about the upcoming surgery and did a very basic neurological check. During the strength testing, he called me a wimp (he was joking), because I was weaker now since I'd lost a lot of muscle. We all knew that I definitely was not a wimp! According to him, I checked out halfway normal, which was great for me being that I was pretty abnormal at the time. I was just glad to be cleared for surgery from his point of view.

The following week mom, grandma, and I went to the Red Cross Blood Donation Center in Toledo where many of the nurses knew me quite well already. I had to donate three pints of blood for surgery but because I wasn't always reliable, mom and grandma also donated because they had a compatible blood type that I could receive. Mom filled up her pint before grandma and I even got started. It took awhile and I was a little woozy at the end, but the job got done, and the three pints were ready to be shipped to the Hospital for Special Surgery after being tested.

That Friday dad got a phone call at work that made him very nervous. The owners of the apartment we were going to rent from in NYC were having family issues and their apartment was no longer available for us.

The consultant through whom we had booked the apartment was in a panic but she pulled a few strings and soon had us rebooked. (Afterward, she told dad she had to have some wine when she first heard the news because she didn't know what to do with only five days before we were to arrive.)

Instead of a one bedroom and one bathroom apartment like we originally were going to have, she got us a two bedroom and three bathroom apartment in a great neighborhood. She said a few famous people had even rented it before. It was quite expensive but because it was a last minute change, the owner of the new apartment was very understanding and lowered the price to accommodate us.

June 7th was my last day at work. I knew that some of the elderly residents I'd grown close to might not be there when I came back a few months later so I stopped by to say goodbye and give hugs to some of them. A few weeks earlier, my coworkers, and other Fairlawn Haven employees had signed cards and donated money to help my family with medical expenses. I couldn't believe the support that I had from them, and it really made my heart swell with love and appreciation.

The next evening my whole family came over for homemade ice cream. I wanted to make sure that we all got together one more time before we left for NYC. Surgery had always seemed so far off but now it was almost time to go. Until I was being wheeled into the OR, I had a hard time believing that this surgery really was happening.

15 New Yorkers

"Have I not commanded you? Be strong and courageous. Do not be terrified; do not be discouraged, for the Lord your God will be with you wherever you go." Joshua 1:9 (NIV)

The night before we left for New York City I didn't sleep well. I kept thinking of what still needed to be packed and done. I was so excited to go but yet sad to be leaving Lenney and my family.

We stopped at my dad's attorney's office early that morning because now that I was 19, I needed to have a living will drafted just in case something happened during or after this next surgery. We had the living will signed and printed within an hour and we were home by 9:00.

That's when things got chaotic. All of us were running around making last-minute arrangements, stuffing last minute items into our luggage, saying good-byes and then we were off at 9:30 am headed for Detroit Airport. Of course I set the security equipment off at the airport because my back brace had metal on it. I had to stand to the side for a body check and my brace had to be tested for explosives. I was so happy when that was over and always dreaded the security checkpoints for this reason.

Our flight was delayed at the last minute due to bad weather in New York. Once we were off the ground I settled back, closed my eyes, and listened to worship songs by Chris Tomlin on my iPod. I was anticipating a major surgery, but I knew that God would hold me close to Him when the pain became very intense. He had blessed me in so many ways already, and I knew He wasn't going to stop now!

Annie was with us and I wanted her to see the New York City skyline when we landed, but it was too cloudy. After we had our luggage in hand we made a few phone calls to my sisters and grandparents and then went out to find a taxi. As we arrived at our rented apartment located in the Upper East Side of Manhattan, we saw the owner of the apartment leaning out of the window a few floors up and waving to us. Once arriving, she gave a tour and made us feel so welcome. We all loved the way the apartment was set up and had a great view of the street below.

We had not actually seen the Hospital for Special Surgery before, since Dr. Boachie's office was a block away. After walking 17 blocks, we made it to the hospital which also had a fantastic view of the East River. After working up an appetite, we stopped for supper and bought some groceries. We were amazed at the high prices of so many items in the grocery stores. It would be cheaper to eat out than cook at home! By the time we got back it was late and we had to unpack and organize our home-away-from-home. I couldn't believe that I had a TV, a computer, and a bathroom in my room. We were all exhausted so everyone went to bed but of course I had to stay up awhile and watch TV from my bed!

I kept waking up throughout the night because of the sounds of city life. There were sirens, cars honking, and trash pick-ups at all hours of the night. There were no birds chirping out my window like at home. The busy morning of June 11th had arrived, and I woke up with butterflies in my stomach as I anticipated all the appointments I was going to have that day, so we were up and on our way by 8:15. This time we took a taxi to the Dr. Boachie's office. Once there, we waited for over an hour and were then told he was still in a meeting and we should come back in the afternoon after my other appointments were finished. So we hurried over to the Hospital for Special Surgery for my next appointment with the internist who would be following up with me after surgery. He examined me to make sure that I was healthy enough for surgery, and luckily I was.

After that, we went for my pre-surgical screening appointment where I had an EKG and chest x-ray done, blood samples taken, and a few other tests. I leaned to my right so much, making it difficult to get a clear chest x-ray. But with the help of a radiologist the technician got the job done. Afterwards we sat and watched the beautiful view of the East River out the window. There were big barges with tug boats that would sail past from time to time. I really hoped that after surgery I would get a room overlooking the river.

Around 2 pm we went back to Dr. Boachie's office. He and his resident sorted through all eleven pounds of my x-rays, and then took pictures of what I looked like in the brace from different angles. He said he would be doing a posterior and anterior approach (incisions made on my front and back) and if I tolerated the first part of the surgery, then he would continue to do the anterior portion as well. Otherwise, the surgery would be divided into two smaller surgeries a week a part. I certainly hoped it would go well because I didn't want to go through two recoveries, which would probably mean a longer hospital stay too.

His plan was to fuse from T-10 to S-1 with screws into my pelvis. He would then remove two to three of my lumbar discs and replace them with cages and fill them in with allograft bone, which is taken from a cadaver, and bone graft taken from my previous fusions. Then he would go from the anterior view and secure everything with more bone graft, and a possible osteotomy, if necessary. Surgery would take approximately eight to nine hours. He seemed very optimistic that he could correct the lean. We had a nice visit and everyone I met that day seemed very nice, which gave me a good feeling for the hospital and also for those who would care for me.

When we walked back out into the waiting room Annie was falling asleep and her struggle to stay awake made us all chuckle. It was a Kodak moment so mom took a picture, even though Annie wasn't too thrilled! It had been a long day for all of us.

Later that evening, after dinner, we took a stroll in Central Park because our apartment was only three blocks away. Just as we were about home it began pouring down rain. We were soaked and exhausted after a busy day of appointments and ready to leap into bed. I really enjoyed having my own room with a TV in it because it helped to keep my mind off of the pain when I couldn't sleep at night, which was quite frequently.

The next day was a bit easier on all of us. We got to sleep in because my first appointment was in the early afternoon. That morning dad and I walked over to Eli's Manhattan, which had a fantastic assortment of breads and gourmet grocery items, and then stopped at a fresh fruit stand on our way home. When we arrived home with our purchases we all had a brunch of bread and fresh fruit.

Then we headed over to see my pulmonologist at the massive New York Presbyterian/Weill Cornell Medical Center. The doctor asked many questions about our family medical history and told us that my overall pulmonary function was at 68 percent, which passed for surgery. After he finished examining me, he wanted to know a little bit about Ohio, since he'd never been there before. It was a very quick appointment.

Then we were free for the rest of the day so we decided to take the subway to Ground Zero. It was amazing to see the progress that had been made since the previous time we were there, nearly five months earlier! On our way back we took the wrong subway and ended up far from home and in a place where little English was spoken, but the locals were helpful and soon we found the right subway to take us back to the apartment.

The next day was completely free. Dad and I brought home fresh bagels for breakfast and then we headed out to see the Empire State Building. It was a fairly chilly day and cloudy, even though it was mid June. Even so, it was an amazing view from up top. It was so neat to see what life looked like from the 88th floor. Cars were like little bugs crawling along.

Then we went to St. Patrick's Cathedral where a wedding was taking place. The cathedral was huge and absolutely gorgeous. By then I was getting really tired so I suggested we go back for an afternoon nap. As we walked home it started to rain outside. Luckily, this time we were prepared and had our umbrellas!

We had supper at a neighboring restaurant that evening and then we turned in early. I was still having trouble sleeping through the night but luckily there was always something good to watch on my TV.

The next day we woke up to a relaxing morning. Around noon we went out and bought city bus tour tickets. It was a chilly, windy day but we still sat on the top of the double decker bus so we could have a great view. We got off at Chinatown, which was like a whole new world. There were many outdoor markets with everything you can think of for sale. Then we walked through Little Italy where there were blocks of restaurants with seating outside. I felt as if we'd traveled from China to Italy. We took the bus tour all over the city that day and saw so many sites that we otherwise wouldn't have even known about!

We came home around 5:30 to rest and Dad and Annie went out to get us supper. We were really enjoying the apartment and it didn't take long until it really felt like home. We loved the neighborhood, our neighbors, and the doormen. I just wasn't too fond of the early morning noisy trash pick-ups!

That evening we took the subway to Times Square. It was packed with people! You could keep walking and never quite see everything! All the colored, flashing lights were so pretty. It's a place that you see on TV, but when you actually see it in person, it is hard to believe. Of course we had to take Annie to the giant M&M store that has any kind of color and type of M&M that you can think of.

The next day we took the city tour bus to Battery Park. Inside the park lies a huge sculpture that was in the courtyard of the World Trade Center and, although it's very battered and twisted, it still has its general form. Beside it is a flame that is always burning to remind us of those who lost their lives on September 11, 2001.

Then we got in line for the ferry to Liberty Island. It was a cold ride. Seeing the Statue of Liberty up close was really amazing - it's so big! And to think it was one of the first things our ancestors saw when they arrived in America.

The next morning, Katie and Derek flew in from Ohio and Annie and dad went to pick them up at the airport. While they were gone, mom and I decided to be brave and took the subway to the Empire State Building and bought hoodies because it had daily been so cold and rainy. We came home to a full apartment. Once everyone got settled we took a walk to the nearest fire station, Engine Company 22, Ladder Company 13, 10th Battalion, so Derek could inspect the equipment and have a tour of the station since he is also a firefighter. There were many cute firemen that is for sure! Then we returned to Rockefeller Center and Times Square for Katie and Derek to see.

That evening we had an early Father's Day celebration and gave dad some gifts because I would be in the hospital and Annie would be back home in Ohio on that day. Annie also got me a really cute duck that she couldn't wait to give me, to make me smile while I was in the hospital. We all went to bed in good time because it would be a very early morning.

In the weeks and months before this surgery, I felt a nervous excitement for this surgery. June 17th always seemed so far off, but now it was almost here. I went to bed at the normal time that night but I couldn't sleep, so I'd watch TV, sit on my windowsill, or do some sit ups because I knew those days would be over after surgery. Every time I would lie down and attempt to sleep, my stomach would start churning and I felt sick. I felt something was going to happen but I couldn't pinpoint it. The only thing that seemed to help and comfort me was to pray. **This was an excerpt from my spiritual journal reflecting these thoughts. *Sweet Jesus, whatever happens; I find comfort in knowing that You have always loved me throughout my many situations and circumstances. You are a beautiful and caring Father, and I long to be a pure reflection of Your love so that I may touch those I come in contact with every day with Your everlasting and abounding love. I love You Jesus!*** I finally turned the TV back on and then got on Facebook around 2:00 in the morning. I'm sure people were surprised when they saw what time I e-mailed them. I was still awake when mom got up after 3am and then around 4, after having no sleep and with my adrenaline pounding, I took my shower and I enjoyed every bit of that shower because who knew when the next one would be. *Libbey, I have everything under control, Jesus*

A Sister's (Rebekah) Perspective

Little did we know that her one surgery to correct her scoliosis would turn into many over the years. Over time there were more complications, more unknowns, many doctor appointments, and more procedures done. It's been hard to see Libbey go through all this. You ask the questions Why her, When is she going to be "fixed," and When will there be the miracle we have all been praying for? It seems that so many people had been continuously praying for this nightmare to be over for her. So why hasn't it happened? That is a question I have struggled with. But through all this, all the ups and downs, Libbey has remained so strong, within herself, as well as in her faith. Her faith seems not to be shaken at all. Instead, it seems to have only gotten stronger throughout all this. I'm not sure I could have remained so strong in a situation like this. Libbey has taken this negative situation life has thrown at her and has turned it into a positive. She has impacted so many people on her journey, whether it is nurses, doctors, friends or family. She has remained so strong in her faith and her faith just continues to grow. She trusts that God has a plan for her, even though she doesn't know what that is exactly, and is excited to find out what He has in store for her. There's a lot to learn from Libbey. We can learn how to be patient, and trust in God, even when we want answers right now. We can also learn that we don't have to drown in self-pity when times get tough. Everything happens for a reason, right? We may not know what that reason is, but everything happens in God's time.

In January of 2009, we flew to New York City to see another spine
surgeon for his opinion of my case. I was not too excited about going
to NYC at first but it didn't take me long to love the city! This was a
picture I snapped on our way into the city the first time.

Before my fifth surgery, which was scheduled for June 17, 2009, we had to be in the city a week in advance for tests and doctors appointments. Pictured above are Mom, me, Dad, and Annie all standing outside of the Hospital for Special Surgery in Manhattan, NYC.

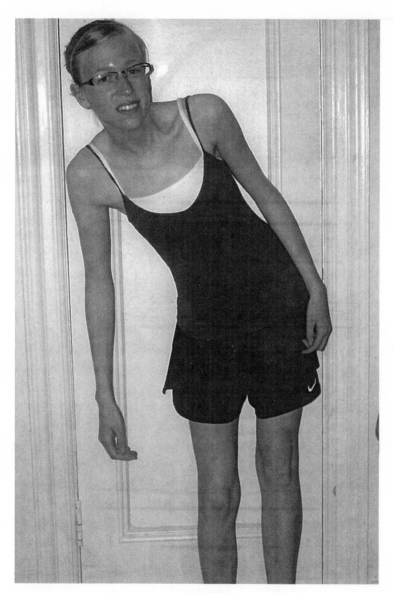

This picture was taken on June 16, 2009, which was the night before my fifth surgery. Without my back brace on I was really leaning forward and to the right, so I was hoping that the surgery would be successful so that I could stand straight again without having to wear my back brace for support.

16 Surgery #5

"The joy of God is experienced as I love, trust, and obey God-no matter the circumstances and as I allow Him to do in and through me whatever He wishes, thanking Him that in every pain there is pleasure, in every suffering there is satisfaction, in every aching there is comfort, and in every sense of loss there is the surety of the Savior's presence, and in every tear there is the glistening eye of God." -Bill Bright

The ride to the hospital was absolutely beautiful and calming outside with the sun rising. Although deep in my stomach I had a sense of dread because I knew the extreme amount of pain I would be in afterwards. *"In Him and through faith in Him we may approach God with freedom and confidence. I ask you, therefore, not to be discouraged because of my sufferings for you, which are your glory."Ephesians 3:12 (NIV)* Before I knew it, we were at the Hospital for Special Surgery.

After arriving, we slowly went up to the 4th floor surgery waiting room, which had big floor to ceiling windows, and a beautiful view of the East River. When we arrived, the sun was rising and the view from the window was absolutely breathtaking! I had to check in at the desk, and then we found a spot to sit that had room for everyone, and a great view of both the river and TV.

Soon I was called back to do some pre-admitting paperwork, and at 6:15 a.m. I was called back into the pre-op area. My room was in the corner and so it had big windows facing the river and the rising sun. While I was changing into my stylish gown, my wonderful nurse was asking me questions from behind the curtain. Then I had to come up with a urine sample, again. I wished that they could just take my word that I am NOT pregnant!

Dr. Boachie came in and spoke with my parents and me. He had decided that it'd be best to break the surgery into two parts. During the first surgery he was going to fuse my spine from T-10 to S-1 with rods and screws and he thought it would last five to six hours. He marked my back to make it clear where the surgery was going to be, answered our final questions, and then went out to get ready. I was feeling very confident, and ready to go. It was so nice to be surrounded and supported by my family. Everyone was there with me but my oldest sister Rebekah, but she called soon before I was taken back to wish me good luck!

After Dr. Boachie left, the dietician, my anesthesiologist, and Dr. Boachie's fellow came in and had to take turns talking to me and asking questions. My poor nurse just wanted to start my IV, but every time she came in, someone else was with me.

One of the nurses who would be with me in the OR came in and introduced herself, and a Physician's Assistant then came in as well and had me sign some important last minute paper work. My nurse was then finally able to start my IV, although it took a few pokes until a successful spot was found.

At 8:30 a.m., my surgical nurse came in, put a cap on my head, unlocked the brakes on my bed, and wheeled me out of my room. We reached the kiss corner and I gave a hug and kiss to each of my family members and then I was wheeled behind the double doors into a hallway that was absolutely freezing. I couldn't believe that I was really having another surgery.

A Father's Perspective

Watching Libbey go down the hall for surgery I have realized that I have to let go and depend on God to see her through it again and again. Will she wake up? Will this surgery work? Will something go wrong and she never be able to walk again? All these thoughts ran through my head.

Dr. Boachie always used OR 12 I was told, and so I was wheeled in, and saw a few people analyzing my x-rays on the far wall. Many people introduced themselves, and told me what their part was going to be throughout my surgery, which was both interesting and reassuring.

They set my bed next to the surgical table and on a 1, 2, 3, lifted me unto it. Looking up I saw the huge, intimidating surgical lights ready and waiting to do their job. Suddenly I got that relaxed feeling and knew that my anesthesiologist was sneaking sedation medication into my IV. My surgical nurse stood by my bedside, rubbed my arm reassuringly and told me that they would take good care of me. The oxygen mask was placed over my nose and mouth, and I was told to breathe deeply, which soon put me to sleep.

Five hours later, Dr. Boachie went out and told my family that he was very pleased with the correction they had achieved with the instrumentation, and so did not go on to perform the osteotomy. My parents had to wait a few hours until they could see me in the PACU, which is where I stayed over the next few days.

A Sister's (Annie) Perspective

On the morning of Libbey's fifth surgery in New York City, I woke up with an awful cold and headache. This did not make the mood of the day any better. The day is blurry in my mind because I felt so awful, but I do remember Dr. Boachie coming out to say that everything went fine during surgery, which was what I wanted to hear. Unfortunately, in the PACU at the Hospital for Special Surgery, they have a strict policy that no one under 14 years of age was allowed to go in to see patients, even though I was turning 14 the next month. So the next few days I had to sit for what seemed forever and saw many re-runs on the TV. Finally, the day before I was to come home to Ohio with my sister and brother in law, my dad went for his short visit and convinced the nurses to let me come see her. Seeing her made me feel so much better, because I was able to say goodbye before I left, even though I'm not sure if she even knew I was there!

The day after surgery I had an episode that I only remember vaguely. I was moaning and my heart rate jumped really high. My hands and feet went stiff and clamped up and my eyes felt funny. I don't remember much after that besides hearing lots of doctors surrounding my bed and someone calling for a crash cart. I felt trapped inside my own body and was a bit scared. This lasted for a few minutes.

The neurologist later confirmed that I had had a seizure, and later on I was taken down to radiology for a brain MRI. I remember being in an intense amount of pain. With each surgery I always thought that I was prepared and convinced myself the pain wouldn't be too bad, but nothing could ever really prepare me for that kind of agony. The pain was beyond what I could put into words. Luckily they kept me medicated and every few hours the nurses would roll me on my side and prop my back up with pillows to help with circulation.

I stayed in the PACU for four days and then I was moved to the 6th floor. I had an awesome view out my window, according to my parents. I don't know; my eyes were closed most of the time!

A Mother's Perspective

It felt like each time Libbey had surgery, something 'different' always seemed to pop up that struck us as strange, but we just dealt with it and moved on. After her 5th surgery, and the first one to be done in New York City, the 'different' popped up once again. Was it amusing....was it unsettling; yes, a bit of both. This time a few days post-op I noticed that Libbey kept asking me the same questions....again, and again...repetitious yes, amusing yes....she kept asking and I kept repeating the same answers....over and over again. Then one time when we were sitting with her I thought she looked cold so I asked her if she needed another blanket....she always liked mounds of blankets on her bed at home. She was quick to respond 'no, I am fine'. It wasn't 5 minutes later that a nurse walked in and asked her the same question and the response was 'yes, that would be great, I'm cold'. It was a bit unsettling that she didn't even remember me asking her, but we got her covered and warmed up anyway.

Of course I can't forget the morning we went in and she proceeded to tell us how she 'woke' up in summer camp and she and the nurse had a great conversation about it. It had been 6 years since she had gone to summer camp, yet when she woke up that morning, she was sure that was where she was. I'm sure the nurse was quite amused at that conversation, but no doubt was also used to hearing confused patients talk. Then the next day to our surprise, she was shopping at Target, or so she thought! These are just a few of the interesting conversations we had with her!

Two days later a physical therapist helped me sit and then stand. I felt very straight and was quite excited. My parents were disappointed that they weren't there when I stood up for the first time. Later on I was taken down for a lumbar MRI which lasted for quite a while, but I was asleep for most of it.

I also got a very nice roommate who had had her hip replaced. She was quite a talker for someone who just had surgery. That night they got me to eat some ice cream, which was exciting to my family because I hadn't eaten in over a week. But it didn't take long for it to come back up.

The next day my aunt who lives in Washington D.C. took a day trip to NYC to visit me and it was great to have a visitor! She told us a funny story about how she got side-swiped by a taxi and knocked down as she was walking to the hospital. That wasn't a very nice welcome to the city! She was fine; just a little skinned up.

I was really not looking forward to having another surgery the next day but knew it was necessary to ensure that a good correction was achieved on my spine for years to come.

"Let us hold unswervingly to the hope we profess, for he who promised is faithful." Hebrews 10:23 (NIV)

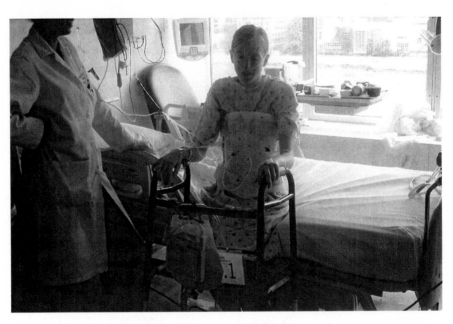

On the morning of my fifth surgery, I found out that my surgery was going to be broken into two surgeries with the second surgery a week after the first one. It was very painful and I was so drugged up that I really don't remember too much the first few days after each surgery.

17
Surgery #6

"Just think, you're here not by chance, but by God's choosing. His hand formed you and made you the person you are. He compares you to not one else-you are one of a kind. You lack nothing that His grace can't give you. He has allowed you to be here at this time in history to fulfill His special purpose for this generation." –Roy Lessin

I woke up on the morning of June 24th, day 7 in the hospital, drugged out, but with my adrenaline flowing. My patient care assistant gave me a quick wash down and I mean quick because I was very unsteady on my feet and dizzy. When I got back to bed, my roommate pulled back the curtain that divided our beds and talked with me, while she ate her breakfast. She told me all about her background and the history of Coney Island and that made her hungry for a Coney dog.

You'd think that by surgery number six, I wouldn't get so nervous anymore. Talking with my roommate helped calm the butterflies in my stomach. Little did she know that God was using her to help comfort me as I awaited another major painful surgery. *"Praise be to the God and Father of our Lord Jesus Christ, the Father of compassion and the God of all comfort, who comforts us in all our troubles, so that we can comfort those in any trouble with the comfort we ourselves have received from God. For just as the sufferings of Christ flow over into our lives, so also through Christ our comfort overflows. And our hope for you is firm, because we know that just as you share in our sufferings, so also you share in our comfort." 2 Corinthians 1:3-5 (NIV)*

I was glad to see my parents that morning because only an hour later, at 11:30, I would be shipped down into the pre-op area again. I wasn't sure why I had to be there two hours in advance since they had all my information from the week before, and my IV was in. My roommate wished me luck as I was wheeled out of the room and down to the pre-op area.

This part of the surgery was new. We were told it was a 129 step surgery and would be done posteriorly which had never been done before. The surgery was traditionally done anteriorly, or through the front, so I was the first one to try out this new procedure, which made my parents a little uneasy. Two to three of my vertebral disks would also be removed and replaced with cages surrounded and filled with BMP (bone morphogenetic protein). He would also use the bone graft from my previous surgeries to secure the cages and screws.

Dr. Boachie and his fellow came in, answered our last minute questions, and then two anesthesiologists come in and introduced themselves to me also. The Physician's Assistant came in next and brought me more paper work to sign. I'm sure it looked nothing like my signature since I was doped up, and did not have my glasses on or contacts in, so I could not see clearly! The same nurse I had the week before in the OR popped her head in also which was nice to see another familiar face, and I knew she'd take good care of me.

A Sister's (Katie) Perspective

Right before your 6th surgery in New York City on June 24, 2009, Dad called me so I could talk with you right before you went into surgery. We had a nice short conversation and I wished you luck. Apparently it was not a very exciting conversation for you, since you don't remember we even talked when asked a few days later! Those drugs they were giving you must have been strong for you to have forgotten about talking with your own sister!

A little past 2:00 p.m., I was taken back to the OR by my surgical nurse. I gave mom and dad a hug and kiss and went through those double doors again, and down the freezing hallway. This time they piled me high with warm blankets before I got super cold, which was good thinking on their part. Then I was wheeled into OR 12 again and greeted by many who seemed to remember me.

My x-ray from the first part of the surgery was hanging up which looked pretty neat. That was the first time I had seen it. I was wheeled right next to the surgical table and then lifted unto it.

They placed cold leads on my chest to monitor my heart, and soon I felt that relaxed feeling come over my body. I was already pretty tired, so when he put the oxygen mask above me and said to breathe deeply, I was asleep immediately.

The surgery took a little over five hours, so slightly longer than expected but it was Dr. Boachie's first time doing this new surgery, so I'd rather him take his time and not forget a step since there were so many!

I vaguely remember when I was in the PACU that night, I always wanted to be rolled over and the nurses kept telling me that they could only roll me every three hours, but I kept asking anyways since I didn't know the time.

Early each morning a nurse and patient care assistant would give me a wash down and change my sheets. I was pretty out of it, but I remember the woman who washed me said I was special to her, like a daughter, so she always saved me for last and gave me an extra special rub down with lotions. I was squeaky clean all over and felt so fresh!

I also continued to have more seizures. I hallucinated and was very repetitive according to my parents. I also had a PICC-line placed in my upper arm to receive IV nutrition since I had gone nearly ten days without eating. My daily blood draws could be taken from my PICC line also, meaning no more needle pokes!

That weekend I was moved back up to the 6th floor again, but this time I did not get the bed with the window view. I slept most of the day and didn't notice, but Mom and Dad really missed the window because they enjoyed watching the boats sail down the river.

My roommate and her husband were very nice. She was a retired art teacher and had just had a double hip replacement, and was recovering nicely. When my parents left each afternoon to eat and take a walk, my roommate's husband always told me to holler if I needed anything. They were such a sweet couple.

On Sunday afternoon, I took a nap just like all the other days while mom and dad were out. When they returned a few hours later, they found me moaning. The nurse couldn't get any response from me so she called a code and the crash cart was by my bed within seconds and ready to be used if needed. When I would have seizures, my heart rate would skyrocket which was why a crash cart was called because at any time my heart could stop because of the stress it was in.

My roommate got out of my room in a hurry according to my parents.

They said they never saw a person with a walker, move so fast! There were at least ten people surrounding my bed within seconds of the code being called and finally they wheeled me back to the PACU because I wasn't responding. There they could monitor me more closely. After forty-five minutes I finally began to respond. It was concluded that I had had another seizure.

The next morning while doing rounds, Dr. Boachie came in when I had yet another seizure. He decided to take me off all pain medications except Tylenol, but luckily for me someone changed his mind, so I got a slightly stronger pain medication. Even so, I didn't come out fully from all the drugs until later that evening and, after nearly two weeks of being on very strong pain medications to getting absolutely nothing, left me laying there in pure agony. I was wide awake and I went from having horrible hot sweats to being freezing cold and very restless.

I was miserable, and kept praying over and over for God to come take me home because the pain was almost more than I could handle and I was ready to be free of my physical pain. I had stayed strong the last few years, and in my moment of weakness I was ready to go to my heavenly home where there would be no more pain and suffering. Why didn't God let my heart stop a day earlier when the code was called for me? Obviously God had other plans in store for me, but that night it was hard to understand that through the intense pain.

I didn't get one wink of sleep and three times during the night I asked a nurse for some pain medication, but I never received any until the next morning when Dr. Boachie's resident and my mom came in. Later on I was taken back up to the 6th floor and got the beautiful window view.

Almost as soon as I got to the floor, my physical therapist popped in after I had just had another hot episode. I was very dizzy and only able to walk to the end of my bed, which was a bit discouraging, but it was a start.

The next day I spoke with my pain management doctor who explained that all the symptoms I was experiencing was due to the drug withdrawal. My body went from having a very high amount of narcotics to practically nothing in such a short period of time. He prescribed for me a slightly stronger pain medication that would bridge the two extremes, and would hopefully help with the hot/cold flashes.

In the afternoon I was taken next door to the New York Presbyterian Hospital for an EEG (electroencephalogram), which would show if I had any seizure activity, but luckily it turned out normal.

The next morning, my mom's friend, Shannon, from work surprised us by flying to NYC for a day visit. She was excited and we were very surprised! I was so miserable and bloated that day that I couldn't even see my toes. I think it had to do with the anesthesia sitting in an empty stomach for two surgeries in a week's time. I walked around and was given all sorts of laxatives throughout the day, which didn't help either.

Since it was obvious I was miserable, I didn't have physical therapy that afternoon which I was so grateful for because I probably wouldn't have been able to fit into my brace with my stomach so bloated. The last thing I wanted to do was put on my brace and have the straps tightened.

Mom and dad had to leave each night at 8:00 according to the hospital policy, and by 9:00 p.m. it would be fairly dark outside. I loved watching the sun set and seeing all the city lights come alive. It was a perfect nightlight and the view was so beautiful and peaceful. Each morning I enjoyed watching the school bus across the way at Roosevelt Island pick up and drop off the kids for summer school. That afternoon when my physical therapist came in, I was determined to walk a long ways and I actually walked down the hallway for the first time without feeling lightheaded! After doing so well, my parents were given permission to walk with me whenever I felt up to it which was great news since walking helped me feel less bloated.

That afternoon, I was taken down for x-rays, and a few days later I got to see them for the first time which looked quite impressive.

Each day my parents would bring small stacks of cards with them for me to open. I couldn't believe the number of cards I received! They said the little mailbox at the apartment was always filled with cards each day. One day I came across a card from my friend, Chelsea. She gave me a good chuckle because she wrote down a whole bunch of funny hospital quotes. It hurt every time I laughed but I just couldn't control myself!

Here are just two of the quotes that made me laugh. *"They say laughter is the best medicine...so go out in the hallway and walk behind other people in hospital gowns!"* I was always so paranoid that I would be flashing people when I would take walks, but in all reality that was not possible because the gowns were so big on me that nothing would ever be showing! *"Not everything about being sick is bad. There are the good-looking doctors...whose yachts you're paying off!"* It seemed I always had the good looking fellows, residents, and physical therapists and it made me care more about what I looked like when I knew they were coming, even though I was pale, skinny, and majorly bloated. I appreciated all the cards that I got and they really helped to brighten my day.

That Friday I had a surprise visit from my friend Rebekah who was staying in Rochester, New York for the summer. She couldn't stay very long because her relatives were waiting for her in the lobby but we did have a good time even if it was limited. Now if I could have gotten my hair washed, the day would've been perfect.

In the afternoon a Mennonite pastor from Brooklyn visited me. He told me lots of interesting facts about the city and pointed out some scenic places from my window. The Silver Cup, which is a major recording studio for many TV shows, was on the other side of Roosevelt Island, but I could see all the letters in bright red! I was very glad he stopped by.

That night I was kind of bored and so mom brought my laptop and we all watched a movie together. Then they helped me get ready for bed before they left. Mom and Dad would leave around 8:30, which was a little late, but I don't think it mattered that much because they never got in trouble!

After they left, my nurse for the night would come in and attempt to start my TPN and lipids which would last for twenty four hours. This normally was quite an ordeal because they needed to find an extra IV pole for me, which was always nonexistent. By the time my line was flushed out and everything properly hung and programmed, it took an hour. Then I could attempt to go to sleep.

July 4th came and I felt sad because I had been so sure I would have been out of the hospital by then. The hospital was fairly quiet that day because many patients had been discharged before the holiday weekend, which was nice because the nurses had more time to talk. Some of the nurses brought in snacks to celebrate the holiday. My favorite nurse sneaked me a cup full of party mix and, when I finished it, she filled it up again!

After being cooped up in air conditioning for so long I really wanted to go outside and feel the sunshine on my face. Since there weren't many patients, the unit clerk took us outside after my IV's had been stopped. It felt heavenly and warm, finally some fresh air! I sat in my wheelchair and watched the cars go by. He let me stay outside for thirty minutes, which was a real day brightener.

Throughout the day we watched boats of all colors and sizes cruise down the river, which was fun to watch and made me glad that I had a window view. To celebrate the Fourth of July, mom and dad brought in my favorite ice cream (butter pecan), my favorite fruit (blueberries and strawberries), and chocolate chip cookies. All I could think about the day before was chocolate chip cookies. My parents didn't think that finding a chocolate chip cookie would be so hard, but after going into many bakeries, they finally found some! We munched away happily as we watched a movie. Later on, we took a long walk, making many laps around the whole floor and since there weren't many patients, the charge nurse allowed my parents to stay until 10:30 that night so we could watch some fireworks together. Typically the big firework display was on the East River, which would have been a perfect view for us, but that year the main display was on the Hudson River. We saw some great fireworks from Queens. What a great way to end the night!

The next morning as I was getting dressed with the help of an aide my friend Rebekah stopped by again to say goodbye before she took a bus back to Rochester, NY. It was very nice to see and talk with her again!

That afternoon since the weather was gorgeous; the unit clerk came in my room and asked if I wanted to go out for some fresh air again. Of course I wanted to go out, and I think he did too! Being outside really lifted my spirits and made being inside all day more bearable. That day, I was slowly being weaned off of my IV TPN and lipids. I was told that my nurse couldn't stop them all at once but had to do it gradually so my blood sugar wouldn't be affected.

The next morning, I was so excited because there was a chance that I may be able to go home. I was taken off the TPN completely, and if my blood sugar was normal later on that day, then I was told I had a chance of going home. The day was going so slow, so to break it up we took many walks.

I'm sure I gave everyone at the nurses' station a good chuckle as we kept making laps. Many times, people at the desk would wave and tell me that it was so good to see me with my eyes open. They obviously knew me and had played a part in my care, but I had no clue who they were!

I got my hopes up too high because later on when checked, my blood sugar was too low, even though I had some juice just minutes earlier. I was extremely disappointed because I just wanted to go home. I kept reminding myself that it was only one more night. We kept running into the same housekeeping man while walking, who every time he'd see me, which was quite often, would shout out "hi Miss Ohio". This was funny and made me laugh, which was exactly what I needed to do.

The next morning I kept waiting and waiting and finally Dr. Boachie came in and told me that I could go home. I was so excited! After three weeks of being in the hospital, I was free. My nurse had to go over a lot of paperwork and take out my two IV lines, which hadn't been used in a while anyways. Then Dr. Boachie's Physician Assistant came in to remove my PICC line. It didn't hurt, but was a long tube to take out since it went all the way into my heart. As they wheeled me down to the lobby I said goodbye to my nurses and patient care assistants. Then we were off to the apartment in a taxi.

It felt so good to be back out in the real world after being in the hospital for so long, although I was skinny, pale, and wore the brace that went all the way down to my ankle on the right side. Wearing the brace out in public got me plenty of stares from passerby's walking past and many who asked thought that I'd had leg surgery.

When we got to the apartment, I first wanted to take a stroll down the block a little ways because the sun on my face felt amazing, and I could have used a little color since I was so pale! I certainly was tired and slept the whole afternoon. Laura, the apartment owner, brought Chinese food for us to eat that evening, which was very nice, and better than the hospital food, although HSS did have very good food! It was nice to sleep in an actual bed again, and have a TV.

Each day we would try to get out for two main walks - one in the early afternoon with ice cream as my incentive and then an evening walk when it was cooler. I needed to build up my muscle tone again.

That Saturday, dad left in the morning to head home, making me so sad. I even shed some tears when the taxi pulled up and I had to give him one last hug. I didn't expect that I would cry. One look at me and the taxi driver told dad to take his time. After they pulled away, mom and I walked over to Central Park and found a bench there near a man playing his guitar. That afternoon at nap time I found a bag of gummy bears and a note from dad hidden under my pillow, making me tear up again.

While I rested, Mom went to Eli's bakery and bought us some dark chocolate almonds and peanut butter malt balls. Little did she know how expensive they were until the cashier rang them up and told her it was thirty-six dollars! She almost had a heart attack, but they were so delicious! I also received a package from the doorman that afternoon. Katie and Derek had sent me roses to brighten my day!

A Sister's (Katie) Perspective

In July of 2009, when Derek and I found out that you would finally be able to leave the hospital and get to go back to the apartment with Mom and Dad, we knew we had to send you a little pick-me-up to make your day a little brighter. We looked long and hard at many arrangements of flowers at proflowers.com. We both decided on a little arrangement with many different colored roses. We both thought that it was bright and cheery and hoped it would put a smile on your face when you got it. Lucky for us, we picked well and found out later that we were the ones that got you your first banquet of roses!

On Sunday morning some relatives who live on Long Island came to visit. I had not met some of them before, and mom had not seen them in many years, but we had such a great time sharing stories and many laughs. Later that afternoon we walked in Central Park. It was such a nice day so we kept walking and mom kept asking how I was feeling and I'd always say just fine. I was fine until I realized we had to turn around and go back. I tried to focus on that bowl of ice cream I would get when I made it back to the apartment. Anytime there was an unoccupied bench we'd stop and sit for awhile. An older man walked past with his dog, stopped, and said I looked like I needed to pet his dog. I really did! By the time we got back to the apartment I was so tired I thought I was going to die. I never made that mistake again!

On Tuesday, my grandpa arrived to stay with us for the last few days. He was originally from Queens so he felt quite at home. Grandma had been asking us if we needed him to bring anything and all I could think of was chocolate chip cookies. Grandma baked, and carefully packaged some for Grandpa to bring. They tasted delicious! One morning when grandpa was coming back from his morning walk he found a package outside our apartment door with my name on it. Inside was a card from our favorite doorman. He gave me an assortment of NYC shirts, postcards, and a clock shaped like the Statue of Liberty. It was so thoughtful, and we were certainly going to miss him!

During the nights, I would stay up and watch TV, because it was hard for me to get into a comfortable position. I also liked sitting on the windowsill with my window open to listen to the peaceful sounds of the city at night and feel the breeze on my face. I was getting a bit discouraged because I was beginning to lean again.

A few days later I had a final post-op exam before going home. Dr. Boachie had a meeting out of town so I saw his fellow. They took x-rays and some photos and we were told to come back in three months.

Since it was our last day in NYC I wanted to walk all the way back to our apartment, which was seventeen blocks. We did have to stop many times to rest, but we made it.

That night I did get quite upset. I told mom that I went through all that pain only to look not much different than before the fifth surgery. We decided that what we really needed was some fresh air, and so we took a final walk around our neighborhood. I was going to miss it there so much, but was ready to see my family and Lenney again. *"Dear Lord, when I am filled with uncertainty and doubt, give me faith. In the dark moments of life, keep me mindful of Your healing power and Your infinite love, so that I may live courageously and faithfully today and every day. Amen"*

The next morning we had to get up fairly early because we had a 9:30 a.m. flight out of LaGuardia. The security people were very impressed with how much I set the alarms off, and after being body searched and tested, I was cleared.

The flight was on schedule and I slept most of the way back to Detroit. There was Annie and dad waiting for us and Annie and I were wearing the exact same shirt and we hadn't even planned it!

It was almost creepy how quiet it seemed when we first got home because all we heard were bugs. I had gotten used to the horns and sirens in the city. Lenney was happy to see me. Later that evening both of my sisters came over with flowers and balloons. It felt so good to see them again. A week later I started physical therapy because I was beginning to lean again.

One thing I really struggled with after getting out of the hospital was my intense desire, while in the PACU, for God to take me home. I told my parents one night that I was ready to go to my heavenly home, and days later, I felt really guilty because I felt as if I was giving up. Many have told me that it was only rational to have those thoughts since I was in an extreme amount of pain. Who wouldn't want to escape the pain? I was still alive and breathing so God was not finished with me yet on earth, and I was eager to see what else he had in store for me. Every time I would think back to that night in the hospital, I felt guilty and it took time to get over that guilt, and realize that the thoughts were only natural given the situation I was in.

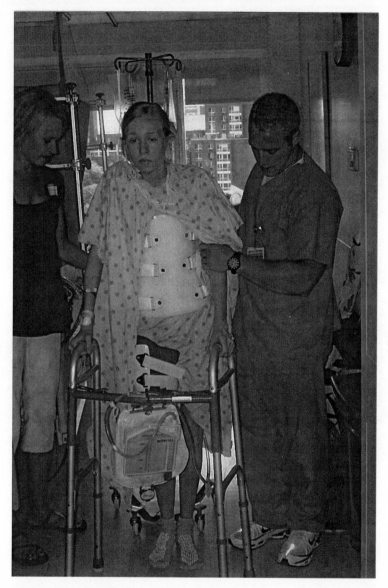

I had physical therapy two times each day when I was in the hospital, which wasn't always my favorite time of the day, but I had great physical therapists.

I was so fortunate to have the side of the room with the window view. As you can see, I had a great view, and the sunrises were absolutely breathtaking each morning. I was usually up very early as the resident or fellow would typically be in to see me anywhere from 4:45 to 6:00 a.m.

18 Appointments, Appointments

"I trust in God's unfailing love forever and ever. I will praise You forever for what You have done; in Your name I will hope, for Your name is good." Psalm 52:8b-9a (NIV)

On August 6th, I had an appointment with Dr. Munk in Toledo. Everyone was glad to see us again. When looking over my medication list, Dr. Munk was very concerned about the amount of Tylenol I was taking and told me that my liver would eventually shut down if I kept taking the same amount of Tylenol. I knew that I was taking too much, but at the time, Tylenol seemed to be the only thing to help a bit with the pain. He really wanted me to go back to the pain management doctor to see if something could be done to help the pain because he wanted me to stop taking so much Tylenol.

I saw the pain management doctor the next week. He decided to try a different type of injection, but he needed to see where I was fused to determine his course of treatment. When he turned on the x-ray machine the first words out of his mouth were "holy Moses." Because of the location of the instrumentation he couldn't do the injections he had hoped to try. Instead, he started me on a medication that I was to take three times a day, to see if that would help and, if not, he would try more of the same injections he had done before.

Towards the middle of August I began vomiting nearly every day and I didn't know why. I was fine in the morning and afternoon, but after eating supper I would vomit multiple times.

My second year of college began on August 20th. Being that I couldn't sit for very long and it was a little difficult to concentrate due to pain, I took one class. I was scheduled to take a second night class but I had been throwing up every night, so after many tears, I decided to drop that class. I felt as if my body was winning which made me so frustrated. I really wanted to take more classes at college, but on the flip side we weren't even sure if I'd be able to take any classes at all, so at least I was able to take one class.

Two weeks later I saw a gastroenterologist at the Cleveland Clinic. Because I had been vomiting quite frequently she prescribed that I have a hydrogen breath test series, just to be sure I wasn't allergic to any foods. On our way out I made the appointments for the hydrogen breath testing. The tests needed to be done on three different days, since I had to be on an empty stomach.

I had an appointment with a seizure doctor also at the clinic that afternoon. He looked at my EEG results and the MRI's of my brain that had been taken two months earlier in New York. He did a physical exam, and then said he didn't think I had epilepsy but wanted me to have a sleep deprived EEG done just to make sure. He set up a plan for me to slowly get off my seizure medication, which I was taking daily, and scheduled an EEG for when we came back in two months.

Later in September, I went back to see the pain management specialist in Toledo because the medication he prescribed wasn't helping, so I stopped taking it. He decided to try the injections again but after a few days I knew the injections hadn't helped with the pain at all. One positive was that I had finally stopped vomiting. We never did figure out what caused the vomiting.

A week later my parents and I went back to the Cleveland Clinic for my first round of the hydrogen breath testing. I wasn't allowed to eat anything until after the test which started at 1:30. All I had to do was drink a huge glass of a glucose solution, and then over the next three hours I was monitored to see if any of my hydrogen levels increased which could indicate a possible allergy to substances with glucose.

Every 15 minutes after drinking the solution I had to blow in a special bag so the hydrogen concentration could be measured. At the end of my three hours, my levels had not increased.

Two days later we went back for the second round. This time I drank a large glass of a fructose solution and every fifteen minutes for three hours my hydrogen levels were monitored. My levels did increase slightly during this test but were still within normal limits.

Since I had another round of testing the next morning, we stayed the night in the city. That evening while we were taking a walk we met a man selling Cleveland Cavalier pre-season tickets on a street corner for only ten dollars. We had to buy them because we liked the Cavs! So off we went to the game. Our seats were only five rows from the top but what a view. We had a great time but decided to leave as the fourth quarter began because it was getting pretty late and the next morning I had the final round of testing.

The next morning I had to drink a cup of lactose solution. I must say it wasn't easy to get this down because the mixture would not mix and was very gritty. I had to plug my nose so I wouldn't gag. My nurse got a chuckle out of that and told me that I wasn't the only one to plug my nose! Every thirty minutes for three hours my hydrogen levels were monitored. I tested normal for this test also. Back home we went and we were still no closer to finding the source of my gastro problems.

The following week I went to Toledo for a second round of pain injections. I laid down on my stomach, which was always so uncomfortable for me because it made my lower back hurt. The procedure was a little painful but I never said a word the entire time, just bit my lip. I kept telling myself that, with all that I'd been through, a few injections should be a piece of cake.

I didn't feel any immediate relief and so the doctor told me there was nothing more he could do for me. He said I should just keep doing what I was doing for pain management. This was discouraging, because nothing really was helping and I wanted to stop taking pain medication.

* * *

On October 10, 2009 we were off to New York City again. Our flight landed in NYC just after noon so we had the whole afternoon to ourselves. After lunch at our neighborhood diner, Blooms, we walked to St. Vincent's Hospital, which is where many people were taken after 9/11. There is a tribute on the fences opposite the hospital that hold hundreds of tiles that were painted and decorated by people all over the world to honor those who lost their lives.

That night we walked to Times Square because it was so nice outside and our hotel was very close by. We had an awesome view of the Empire State Building from of our hotel window.

The next morning, we took our time and when we were all ready we walked to Grand Central Station where we took the subway down to Ground Zero. We were amazed by the progress they had made in just a few months. From there we walked along the Hudson River all the way to Battery Park. The view was fantastic, especially with the sun shining down on the water making it sparkle. Then we walked across the Brooklyn Bridge and the view of the skyline was incredible!

133

On our way back we stopped in Central Park and then, instead of taking the subway back to our hotel, we walked back up 5th Avenue. We had fun window shopping in the many very unaffordable stores. It was an exhausting day of sightseeing so we were ready for bed when we reached the hotel that night.

There was no taking our time the next morning. Before my morning appointment with Dr. Boachie we had scheduled a time to meet with the Director of Nursing at HSS to discuss some concerns about my hospital stay that past summer. She thanked us for taking time to give feedback on our experience to help them make changes as needed.

Then it was back to Dr. Boachie's office where I was taken back rather quickly, and didn't really have time to get nervous! I had to have new x-rays taken first. The x-rays didn't look right to us but Dr. Boachie explained that it was because my spine was slightly rotated which made the screws just appear out of place. He showed me how to do several exercises in the exam room and wanted me to come back in six months.

We all left feeling a bit discouraged. I had had two major, painful surgeries nearly four months earlier and I was still leaning and wearing my brace all the time. I had to wonder what my future would hold. Would I be wearing a back brace for the rest of my life? Would more corrective surgery be necessary? One of my favorite songs by Jeremy Camp called "Healing Hand Of God" popped into my head. *"When you feel that there is not anyone, who understands your pain, just remember all of Jesus' suffering. I have seen, the healing hand of God, reaching out and mending broken hearts. Taste and see the fullness of His peace, and hold on to what's being held out; the healing hand of God!"* Physically I had a long way to go to be healed, but God was really working through my heart spiritually. When dealing with trials and disappointments, He was the one who gave me the strength I needed to go on in hope that one day I would receive healing, in his timing.

We decided to walk back to the hotel instead of taking a cab because it was only thirty blocks away, which really isn't that far. We stopped many times along the way to look inside little shops and we found a huge candy store that had everything imaginable and tasty in it! It was late by the time we reached the hotel so we kicked back, relaxed, and watched TV for awhile. But then we decided that since Times Square was only three blocks away we should go see it one last time because we'd be leaving the next afternoon. It was cold so on the way back we stopped at a little shop and dad treated all of us to some delicious hot chocolate to keep us warm.

The next day we had an afternoon flight so we took our time getting ready and packed in the morning. Then we walked with our luggage in hand to Grand Central Station to buy bagels, challah bread, and black and white cookies (sugar cookies with half chocolate frosting and half vanilla frosting on top), to take home to surprise everyone in our family. From there we hailed a taxi to take us to the LaGuardia airport.

Of course I set off the alarms because of the metal in my back brace and had to be body searched. The woman who checked me said she had mild scoliosis and a few weeks earlier her dad had had a spinal fusion surgery in the city. What a neat encounter that was!

There was plenty of turbulence on our flight home. I had my iPod playing worship songs to help me relax. I was feeling very discouraged because I was going home with no real explanation as to why I was still leaning without my brace. I was tired of having no energy, wearing my brace all the time, and being in pain. I knew God would provide me with the daily strength I needed and would comfort me when I was unable to sleep because of pain. I needed to fully trust in Him because He would heal me in His time. Whether it would be a physical healing, I didn't know, but He had my life in his hands. Since I was still living and breathing, God had some major plans for my life yet, that I knew for sure!

I think our bagels smelled up the entire plane. I was so tempted to eat one, but they all made it back home safely without any missing!

Even though it was late by the time we got home, Lenney was there with his wagging tail and slobbery kisses. My family members were more than happy to get the cookies and bagels, because there's no bagel in Ohio that comes even close to a NYC bagel!

* * *

A few days later we went back to the Cleveland Clinic for my gastroenterology appointment. All of my previous tests had come back within normal limits, which was a relief, but I had hoped to figure out why I was so nauseous and vomited so much. Because my GI tract wasn't moving my food along as it should, my doctor wanted me to have a sitzmark test done, along with an abdominal x-ray and blood work. They also scheduled an endoscopy just to check my stomach and esophagus. On our way out of the clinic, we crossed paths with the greeter dog that was an English mastiff. I had never seen such a big dog in my life!

I took the sitzmark test the next day. All I had to do for this was swallow a capsule that had 24 radiopaque circular rings in them. After five days I had to go to our local hospital and get an abdominal x-ray which would show if there were any capsules left in my lower GI tract. This test helps to determine the transit time. Five days later I had an abdominal x-ray to count the markers that remained. Twenty markers were still scattered all throughout my intestines which meant my colon was not working normally. I had to wait for the details until we went back to the Cleveland Clinic in a few weeks.

Over the weekend we went to a University of Michigan football game with a family friend. I had never been to a college football game before so it was exciting and a great way to end the week of having many appointments. We tailgated before the game and then cheered for U of M. They even won the game which was great because they had been on a losing streak!

A week later we went back to Cleveland for my endoscopy. Everything went smoothly until they tried to sedate me. Because of the amount of pain and sleep medication I was on, they had to give me very strong dose of sedatives in my IV before I felt them kick in. Before I knew it, I was in the recovery room and my parents were walking up to see me. That was a very quick procedure. I slept all the way home because I was extremely tired.

I began working at the nursing home again the first week in November. It felt so great to be back and see the residents and my co-workers again. The first day was a bit overwhelming though because there were quite a few new residents that I hadn't met before.

I had to take a day off that week to go back to Cleveland for a sleep deprived EEG that my neurologist had ordered to check for seizure activity. For the test to be accurate, I wasn't allowed to sleep very much the night before. I was very sleepy on the way to Cleveland so, to keep me awake, I watched a scary movie on my laptop.

During the test, electrodes were attached to my scalp and connected to a computer. The tech then turned down the lights and I had to keep my eyes closed while he did some tests with light. After that portion of the test was over, he gave me a blanket and told me I should rest for an hour while he continued to watch my brain waves to see if there was any indication of seizure activity. Of course I couldn't really relax or fall asleep because he was sitting right next to me. Luckily my hair was not all greasy afterwards like it was when I had had a similar test before.

That afternoon I had an appointment with my seizure doctor. He told us my EEG was normal and if I ever had a seizure again, I should come back to see him, but it wasn't necessary to make another appointment. I was very glad because that was one problem I could check off and one less doctor to visit.

In mid-November we went back to the Cleveland Clinic to see the orthopedic surgeon we had seen the year before, for his opinion of my case because I was still leaning. As soon as he came in my exam room he acted annoyed. He didn't know why we were in to see him because he said that there was nothing he could do to help, after not even seeing my appearance out of the brace. We weren't asking him to do anything, we just wanted his opinion. Instead, he said I might benefit from an intense physical/psychological therapy program that the Cleveland Clinic offered. I didn't really think about it at the time because I was really turned off and frustrated because we had driven a long way to get nothing in return but a bill. We were frustrated at his response and went home very disappointed and not knowing what to do next or even who to see.

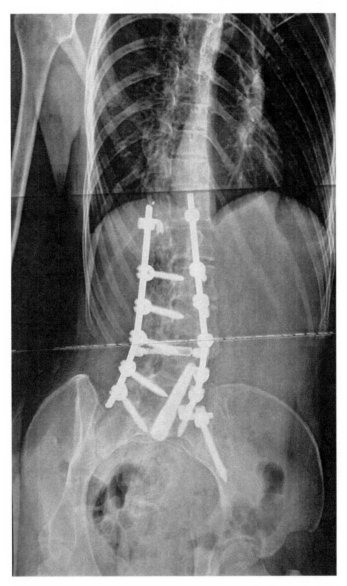

This was an x-ray of what my spine looked like four months post-op. I was still leaning slightly and wearing my back brace all day.

19 Many Miles

"…I tell you the truth, if you have faith as small as a mustard seed, you can say to this mountain, 'Move from here to there' and it will move. Nothing will be impossible for you." Matthew 17:20 (NIV)

A month later we went back to Toledo to see Dr. Munk. After being called back, I was weighed and measured. I had lost six pounds in four months. It was so difficult for me to keep the weight on and losing it made me tired. Then Dr. Munk came around the corner with a big smile on his face and told me to stand up. He shifted me around and checked my reflexes and my overall mobility in different positions. He left the room and later came back with his camera; never my favorite part. So I had pictures taken again from all different angles. Then we sat and talked for a while with none of us being able to come up with an explanation for my leaning.

As frustrating as it was for me, I knew Dr. Munk was equally as frustrated by the way he rubbed his eyes and forehead. It was fairly late when we left because we were there for two and a half hours. I knew I just needed to keep waiting patiently for healing, and keep doing my strengthening exercises daily.

On January 5, 2010, we were back to Cleveland again for my gastroenterology appointment. It was snowing and the roads were a bit slick. I must have been the last patient of the day because nearly everyone had left the office, and the lights were dimmed before my name was called. My doctor said there were too many markers left in my colon when I had the sitzmark test and it seemed I had colonic inertia, which means the nerves and muscles in my colon do not work normally. She thought perhaps the surgeries I'd had contributed to this. She also said she didn't want to scare me but the only real way to correct colonic inertia is to remove the colon. She said I wasn't yet at that point but in years to come I might need to have it removed.

The next day we went up to St. Joseph Hospital in Ypsilanti, Michigan to the Michigan Brain and Spine Institute and ask another orthopedic surgeon there for his opinion of my condition. By this point I was so tired of seeing doctors and I was worried that he would have more discouraging news for me.

I had to have x-rays taken first, and my parents analyzed the x-rays while waiting. I heard feet outside my door, making my heart beat faster. Then the door knob turned, and in walked the very nice doctor. He checked me over from head to toe and concluded that I probably needed an osteotomy performed in the lumbar region of my spine. He hoped I could see Dr. Boachie sooner than my scheduled appointment in March. He also wanted me to have another myelogram/spinal tap done to check that the nerves in my spine and hips were okay because I still had a considerable amount of pain.

Well, strangely enough, Dr. Munk and Dr. Boachie also agreed that it would be beneficial for me to have the myelogram/spinal tap done, so the procedure was scheduled for January 27th at the Toledo Hospital.

I couldn't understand why I had to be at the hospital two hours in advance because I didn't even need an IV. I had two nurses and they both thought I looked so familiar. My doctor came in to explain the procedure. Then I was taken back to the fluoroscopy procedure room and I laid down on my stomach on the exam table. While waiting for the doctor to come in, they began laying the instrumentation out for the procedure. I'd wished that my head was facing the opposite direction when they did that, because the size of the needle was huge and there were multiple ones. Needles normally never bother me but these were big.

He started out by taking multiple x-rays to determine where the best location was to inject. He injected a numbing medication into the area and then inserted a needle to collect my spinal fluid. It took awhile for the spinal fluid to fill up the vials. It was relatively painless, but then again I was pretty immune to pain. Then they injected a dye. When it was over the techs were amazed that I hadn't even flinched throughout the procedure.

I was then wheeled down to CT. I had to lie with the head of the bed tilted down so the dye would go into my upper spine as well. Then I was taken in to a room for a five minute scan. Everything came back normal with no swelling at the injection site. We then went home and for the rest of the night I had to lay down as much as possible to prevent a spinal headache from occurring.

A few days later we went back to the Cleveland Clinic for another gastroenterology appointment. The doctor talked a little about me using a feeding tube, which would be an NG (nasogastric) tube that I would put down my nose and into my stomach at night while I slept to give me some nutrition. But she wanted to try another appetite stimulant medication first. I just wanted to gain some weight so I would have some energy and not have to use a feeding tube.

A few days later I got the prescription filled and took the dosage before I went to bed as prescribed. The next morning I woke up and was so weak that I couldn't even lift the covers off my bed. It was a little scary because my body felt like lead.

I finally got enough strength to get up and make lunch for dad. When he came home, I told him how I felt and went right back to bed and slept until suppertime. My parents were getting worried so they woke me up. I wasn't exactly sure how this medicine was supposed to help my appetite when it put me to sleep all day. I cut the dosage in half but I still had the same symptoms in lesser form and it wasn't helping me to eat, so I stopped taking that medication.

At the end of March my parents and I left for New York City again to see Dr. Boachie. I was quite anxious by then because I was hoping so much that he could figure out a different approach to fix me. I was still leaning and wearing my back brace all day.

My new x-rays showed no change in my spine but I was still leaning significantly. Dr. Boachie and his assistants huddled around my x-rays, taking measurements, and calculating the results. He finally acknowledged there was indeed a problem but he wanted to wait six more months before deciding if more surgery was necessary. In the meantime I was to begin physical therapy again. It was an encouraging appointment.

Our flight home was delayed because of bad weather but we made it home late that night.

A few days later I began physical therapy on Tuesdays and Fridays. With the therapy I was more motivated and determined than ever to stand straight again. I was tired of wearing my brace all the time. At first I didn't notice anything different but after a few weeks of strengthening exercises, I began to feel straighter and then I was starting to be hungry again. I was getting excited but I didn't show my family what I looked like without my brace until I was sure I was really improving and not just thinking I was.

About this time I began praying and looking online for a summer Christian service project somewhere in the United States because I was ready to get out and do something! I knew that health wise I wasn't in the greatest shape yet, but who knew when I would be. I was just looking for some opportunities. The first website that popped up in my search engine was the Campus Crusade for Christ summer project program. I clicked on the site, and the more I read, the more excited I got. There were many places in the United States where they had service projects but one in particular held my interest: New York City. I love the city but the only time I was ever there was for doctor's appointments. I felt as if the city had given me hope, physically, and now I wanted to give back to it spiritually.

I knew this was going to be a real step of faith, and telling others who may not know Jesus about my faith would be difficult, but I knew that if this was what I was supposed to do, God would give me the words to speak. I was really excited and signed up for more information and then the details just started to fall into place.

Two weeks later, I was accepted into the Campus Crusade program in NYC and I began my fundraising. All of the money that I needed for the summer had to be raised, which was hard for me to do because I really don't like asking people for money. I thought that it was going to be very difficult and I just kept praying and thinking that if that was what God really had planned for me to do, then God would provide, and provide He did.

Within two weeks of sending out my support letters I had received all the money I needed, plus an extra one thousand dollars! My extra money went to help other students pay for their trip. I was so excited and amazed at God's provision. **Excerpt from my spiritual journal. *Jesus, once we invite You into our hearts, so many doors and opportunities are available and open. No matter what our age, our life begins when we find You! Father God You are a tremendous God and I can't ever imagine living my life without You in it! I pray that You will give me the courage and strength to bring others to know You!* **

At the beginning of May I also started doing some of my physical therapy exercises without my brace on. I really wanted to slowly wean myself out of my brace and so, every few weeks, dad would cut down the brace a little lower. I'm not sure what began making me straighter, the intense physical therapy, or all the prayers. I think for certain it was a combination. My physical therapist was great and very encouraging but I also greatly believe in the power of prayer.

* * *

On May 26th I had an appointment with Dr. Munk and I was so excited to see him because I was finally standing fairly straight and had gained a little weight. I even made cookies to take down, but halfway to Toledo I realized that they were still sitting on the counter at home!

Dr. Munk felt that the progress I had made was very encouraging, but stressed that I should keep up with my physical therapy exercises and not let my guard down because three years earlier I was straight also but then began leaning again. I tried not to think of that too much and only focused on standing straight.

It was so nice to see everyone at his office and they were excited to see me looking much better. I couldn't stop smiling after we left that appointment because in the previous five years there were not many appointments that I had made such good progress or left with a good report.

June soon arrived and with that came final preparations for my five weeks in New York City with Campus Crusade for Christ. I was so excited to see what God had in store for me. **Excerpt from my spiritual journal. *Jesus, it is so easy to go through the motions every day, but I don't want to do that. I want to step up and stand out in my faith for You. I want to be on fire for You and filled with passion! I love You with everything that is within me!* ** I love NYC and it was so nice to go and know that I had no doctor's appointments while I was there.

It was my first time flying alone, but I had done it so many times that I wasn't too worried, but I barely made my connecting flight. During the first flight, I kept looking at my watch because I knew we were cutting it close. There were two nice boys sitting behind me who were also my age and making the same connection, so after landing, we all went together and found our gate just in time as they were calling the final boarding call.

I had an awesome summer. There were approximately 120 students and leaders in NYC for Campus Crusade for Christ with five teams that each had a slightly different focus. My team, which included a girl from Russia, worked with international students on the massive New York University and Columbia University campuses.

We had English conversation groups daily, and sometimes went out to lunch with the students so we were able to have more in depth spiritual conversations, but this was sometimes difficult because some students English was very limited. I met so many nice people, and had the chance of being a part of bringing two people to accept Christ, which was a real highlight of the summer.

Some other highlights were passing out sack lunches to the homeless, and sitting and eating with the first one we found, cultural night, which consisted of learning about and then eating at a restaurant from that culture, group Bible studies, and seeing the Macy's spectacular fireworks show on the Fourth of July. I also had tourists come up to me, on three separate occasions, down in the subway and ask for directions, which made me happy because that meant I didn't look like a tourist anymore! One man thought I was French, and another girl came up to me speaking Russian, when really the girl that I was with, and also my roommate at the time, was Russian!

I had great leaders, and many told of their experiences of STINTING (short term international), internationally through Campus Crusade for Christ, while in college. I really became interested, but felt that I should probably finish with my college degree first, but became excited about the idea, because who knows what God has planned. The summer project was just what I needed to recharge me both physically, and spiritually. Whatever God had planned for my life, I was ready to follow his will.

When summer project was over, my parents and younger sister met me in NYC and then we went out to Long Island to visit with some of my mom's relatives, and had a great time, especially playing a game of volleyball together. That night when we made it back into the city, it was nearly midnight. We got off the train at Penn Station, which is close to the Empire State Building.

Jokingly, my mom asked if we wanted to go to the top of the Empire State. I said really? She thought we'd think she was crazy suggesting an idea like that so late at night, but we all thought it'd be great! So we went up to the top and had so much fun, and there was hardly a line to wait which was even better. It was perfectly clear and warm outside.

For me it meant a lot to be up there the night before we left the city because I looked around at the vastness of the city and reflected on all I had done there in the past nearly six weeks. NYC holds such a special place in my heart.

That summer experience truly was life changing for me because not only had I grown spiritually, but I also gained a self confidence that I didn't even know I had, and needed. God was truly working through my heart in many ways that are hard to put into words.

I had booked my flight before my parents did and so they couldn't get on the same flight as me out of LaGuardia, but we were going to meet up in Philadelphia and take the same flight into Detroit. They almost didn't make their connection. The plane was loaded and the attendants were getting ready to close the door. I was beginning to wonder what I'd do in Detroit if they couldn't make it since we lived 1 ½ hours away from the airport, and dad had the keys to the Explorer.

The flight attendants were making final arrangements and to my surprise, my frazzled parents and sister came quickly down the aisle and into their seats. I was so relieved that they made it and they were too!

A week after coming home, I found out that the college I was planning to transfer to that semester in nearby Toledo had put their surgical tech program on hold, which was what I was signed up for. I was frantic but remembered that I had already been accepted into Owens Community College, which was a forty-five minute commute from my house, but they also had my program, I just needed to be accepted into it.

It was late to sign up for classes, but luckily the classes that I needed to take were still available just not at the greatest times during the day. I was excited to start that semester since I really didn't enjoy the experience I had had at the local college where I had been at for two years previously.

Two days before the fall semester began, my parents and I drove down and around the college so that I would have a better feel of what buildings my classes would be in and how to get there. We had also taken Lenney with us too, because he loves long rides.

After driving around the college, we found a good place where Lenney could take a pit stop, so we turned the Explorer off to save gas. When we went to turn it back on, it was completely dead! Luckily a very nice campus policeman was on duty that day and had jumper cables with him. It took a few minutes but finally the Explorer started again, although we really needed a new battery soon.

Since I was attending college at Owen's that semester, we didn't have to pay the policeman anything for helping us, although he told me that if he ever saw me on campus I better have a plate of chocolate chip cookies for him. I thought that was a fair deal, especially since he only worked weekends and I was only there during the week!

In the summer of 2010, I spent five weeks in NYC through Campus Crusade for Christ. My group worked on the New York University campus where we held daily English conversation groups for international students. On the far left is Kimi, who was one of my leaders, and the other two girls were international students studying at the Columbia University.

Here I am pictured with a student from South Korea during my summer in NYC. She had heard of Christianity before but never really knew what it was. After meeting with my leader, Anne, and I for lunch a few times, she decided to accept Jesus into her heart. I was so excited and looked all over the city for a bible that had both Korean and English in it!

20 Follow Me

"For I am convinced that neither death nor life, neither angels nor demons, neither the present nor the future, nor any powers, neither height nor depth, nor anything else in all creation, will be able to separate us from the love of God that is in Christ Jesus our Lord."
Romans 8: 38-39 (NIV)

On Sunday, October 10, 2010 we left for our beloved New York City again. We had a late afternoon flight that went from Detroit to Atlanta and then back up to NYC. I couldn't figure out how that flight was the cheapest when more fuel was used.

The sun was setting when we reached Atlanta and was absolutely breathtaking from my plane window. We did not have a long connection at all and even had to change terminals, but we made it with twenty minutes to spare.

Once flying back up to NYC, it was easy to find the major cities, because of the areas of light down below. Another blessing was when we got near the LaGuardia Airport, air traffic was backed up so we ended up circling the city for thirty minutes, which was absolutely beautiful and I wouldn't have minded being up in the air longer. We had never flown into the city at night, so we really enjoyed the view.

After sitting for most of the day, we were ready to walk, so even though it was late after we made it to the hotel, it was warm outside and so we walked many blocks and didn't have to fight any crowds.

Since I had a late afternoon appointment with Dr. Boachie the next day, we went to the Southside Seaport in the morning which gave a fantastic view of the Brooklyn Bridge. The strange thing was that I was hardly nervous at all for my appointment later that afternoon, which was such a nice feeling.

We had to wait a really long time in the waiting room, but after filling out a questionnaire and getting x-rays taken, it was my turn. Dr. Boachie was so pleased with the progress of my overall appearance. I was still not as straight as I could be, but much better than when he last saw me.

While talking we found out that he hadn't had anything to eat since breakfast, and when we asked him how he was making it though the day he pulled out a packet of M&M's from his pocket, and grinned. He said how he had to ration the M&M's each hour, so that they would last him until he went home that night for supper. We were there past 8:00 that night, so he would be eating very late by the time he made it home.

The top of my one rod bulged out in my mid back which caused me pain when I leaned back against a chair, and was especially uncomfortable during school where I had to sit for many hours. It was quite prominent, and Dr. Boachie said that he would be able to go in and shorten that rod, which would be a minor surgery compared to the last two that he did over a year earlier. That made me encouraged and I was hoping it could be done over my winter break. We would be getting a phone call from his secretary the following week with a surgery date. It was a very enjoyable appointment. It was late when we got to the hotel that night, but it was so calm and warm outside so after eating, our "short" walk turned into forty blocks!

The next morning I had to be at the Hospital for Special Surgery early for a lumbar MRI. In order to see the pain management doctor, I had to have a recent lumbar MRI, which seemed a bit crazy. Since I was one of the first appointments of the day, I was taken right back for my scan, and an hour later, I was all finished, which meant that we had much of the day left. I was having an off day though and felt bloated and achy. I just needed some time to rest, and after a few hours my body was recharged and ready to go out again.

Later on that night, I took my parents to one of my favorite places that my roommate and I had discovered that summer in Brooklyn. There is a small park right on the river in Brooklyn that is in between the Brooklyn and Manhattan Bridges that gives a great view of the Manhattan skyline.

We sat on the large rocks near the water for quite awhile and watched the sun set and the lights come on in the city. When looking out at the beautiful city all lit up that night, I just had to reflect on how amazing God is. God gave each of us talents, and to think that God gave some the talent to build huge skyscrapers and bridges to hold up so many people is unbelievable. *"We have different gifts, according to the grace given us. If a man's gift is prophesying, let him use it in proportion to his faith. If it is serving, let him serve; if it is teaching, let him teach; if it is encouraging, let him encourage; if it is contributing to the needs of others, let him give generously; if it is leadership, let him govern diligently; if it is showing mercy, let him do it cheerfully." Romans 12:6-8 (NIV)*

When the wind picked up and we began to get cold, we walked across the Brooklyn Bridge back into Manhattan. There are so many times when deep inside I feel as if this is the city where I will be someday. I don't consider myself a tourist there at all anymore, and it just feels like home.

Two days later we met with the pain management doctor at HSS. It was funny because on our way up in the elevator, the doctor was in there with us and looked very nice. He didn't know who we were, but I knew it was him because I had seen his picture on the internet.

Later on during my appointment, we found out that he was an Ohio State Buckeye fan so we knew he was a good guy! After looking at my films, and doing an exam, he felt that he may be able to help with the pain I was having, and wanted to try doing a different type of injection that I've never had done before. We were thrilled to hear him say that because my last pain management doctor commented that there was nothing more he could do to help me. Of course the injections could not be done at this appointment and wouldn't be able to be scheduled until a few months post-op but he at least gave us some food for thought.

The next day we headed home feeling excited and hopeful, and got to fly into the sunset once again since we had a late afternoon flight. I was reminded of this Bible verse from Hosea 6:3 when looking out my window at the beauty. *"Let us acknowledge the Lord; let us press on to acknowledge Him. As surely as the sun rises, He will appear; He will come to us like the winter rains, like the spring rains that water the earth."* God is so good and will meet our needs according to His timing, not our own which is sometimes easy to forget. Just as the sun rises every day, God is always walking with us daily as well.

A few days after we came home, I met with my advisor at school to help me get some paperwork done so I could apply for the surgical tech program. I was very surprised by what she had to tell me. Since I was going to a community college, the waiting list for the surgical program was three years. My heart sank because I only had one more semester of classes to finish, which would give me two years of no classes until I could begin the program. This was discouraging news for me because since my health had improved, I was able to take more classes and was ready to finish my program.

That night when I was praying, I remembered my leaders from summer project telling me about their Stinting experiences through Campus Crusade for Christ which is for one or two years. Maybe God was telling me that He was giving me a break to do just this before I began the surgical tech program. When I opened my devotions that night, the title was, "Wanted: Disciples."

Then Jesus said to His disciples, "If anyone desires to come after Me, let him deny himself, and take up his cross, and follow Me." Matthew 16:24. Wow! I couldn't believe what I was reading.

After talking with my parents, I decided to apply to stint with Campus Crusade for Christ, and was both excited and nervous about sending my forms in.

Meanwhile, I had two surgery dates in December to choose from - either December 7th or December 28th. The earlier date would be perfect because I'd have plenty of time to recover before the spring semester. The only problem was that it was during my final exam week at school. So I e-mailed all of my teachers to ask if they would let me take my exams early and all but one agreed, so I had to choose the later surgery date.

After we had everything booked, which was rather complicated since we were going to leave the day after Christmas, and be there over New Year's Eve, my teacher e-mailed me back. He said that he would allow me to take my exam early, but not all the information would be covered. By then it was too late, and was the response I wanted the first time I e-mailed him a week earlier, and was wondering why he changed his mind.

We always stayed at the Hotel Bedford in NYC, because it was such a nice hotel, and mom had become friends with the director of Sales and Marketing. So mom sent an e-mail to ask if by any chance there'd still be a room available over the holidays. The director wrote back that they were totally booked but she would see what she could do. By the end of the week we had a room booked for two weeks! So we booked the flights for early afternoon on December 26th because I had three pre-op appointments the following morning.

The weeks flew by, and I was keeping busy by working and going to school. Before I knew it, it was time for final exams. All the stressing and studying had paid off because I passed all my classes with flying colors!

It was hard to get in the Christmas mood because it often seemed so distant. Lights and trees were up, Christmas carols playing, candy made, cookies frosted, and stores were decorated but yet it still didn't seem like it was time for Christmas. I think part of it had to do with us leaving the day after Christmas for NYC, so I was probably thinking more about that.

A Sister's (Rebekah) Perspective

It all comes down to the simple fact that Libbey is an amazing young woman. She has an incredible life ahead of her and yes, I wish there would be answers to so many of the medical questions, but until we get those, or if we ever get answers, we just keep praying for healing. It is an honor to say that Libbey is my sister. I'm so proud of her and everything that she has accomplished and will accomplish. We love you!

Christmas took on a new meaning for me that year as I was reflecting on the many unexpected deaths that occurred in our small community so close to Christmas. As my family gathered around the table for dinner, I looked at each one and silently sent a prayer of thanksgiving to God for allowing us one more holiday dinner together because we just never know when we might be taken up into our heavenly home.

After coming home that night, we heard on the news that a blizzard was set to hit the Northeastern states the next afternoon, Sunday, which would be when we would be flying to New York City with a connection in Baltimore, Maryland. My stomach kept churning as different scenarios played in my head. Sleep did not come easily that night, but I was reminded and comforted by a verse found in Matthew 6:34: *"Therefore do not worry about tomorrow, for tomorrow will worry about itself. Each day has enough trouble of its own."*

Here I am pictured with Dr. Boachie-Adjei who did my last three surgeries in NYC.

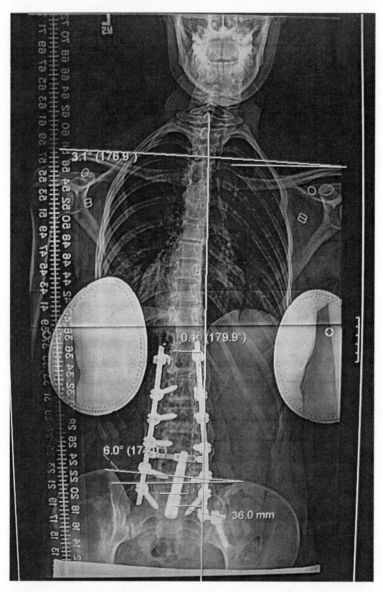

What a beautiful x-ray. I was finally standing straight without wearing my back brace!

21 Surgery #7

"He gives strength to the weary and increases the power of the weak. Even youths grow tired and weary, and young men stumble and fall; but those who hope in the Lord will renew their strength. They will soar on wings like eagles; they will run and not grow weary, they will walk and not be faint." Isaiah 40:29-31 (NIV)

Our alarms all went off early the next morning, December 26th. The first thing I did was check the airline website to see if our flight out of Detroit was still on time. It was! We allowed an extra hour to get to the airport because of the bad weather, and we were glad we did. The roads were horribly icy and we had to go very slow on the turnpike. On our way we saw a lot of accidents and cars in the ditches. I was praying it wouldn't be us.

We jumped the first hurdle in our journey and made it to the airport, although we didn't have that much time to spare! I kept checking our connecting flight status out of Baltimore and it was still on time, although blizzard warnings were out and many flights were being canceled. We were an hour late flying out of Detroit because after we boarded, our plane needed deiced, and had to wait in a long line of other planes. We made it through the second major hurdle of the day once we were in the air.

We arrived very late in Baltimore, and ran through the airport to make our connecting flight. Since we were changing airlines, we had to go through security again, which meant waiting in line, and taking off our coats and shoes. Our carry ons even had to be searched. All we could do was laugh because we were running so late but couldn't do a thing about the setbacks. Once we reached our gate we found that our flight was just delayed.

When we were running through the airport, we passed an Auntie Anne's Pretzel shop that smelled heavenly, so since we were delayed, we had time to get ourselves a yummy cinnamon pretzel. After buying three pretzels, we got a free one. That made our day!

When we returned to our gate, it was beginning to dump snow and visibility got noticeably worse. Just as we finished our pretzels we found out that our flight was canceled.

Our hearts sank but we knew we needed to come up with a plan, quickly. My appointments were to begin at 9:00 the next morning so we had to get to NYC. We considered renting a car, but then we overheard a fellow passenger talking about Amtrak. So while dad was getting directions to the Amtrak station, mom and I got the one checked suitcase. Then we all headed to the shuttle bus to take us to the Amtrak station.

We reached the tiny station and then waited in a long line of other frantic travelers for tickets. The next train into New York City's Penn Station was to leave at 5:45 p.m. which would be a three hour wait but we were so thankful for those tickets.

While waiting, we remembered about that extra pretzel we had gotten back at the airport, and wondered where it was. We concluded that dad must've left the pretzel at the information desk since we were all a bit frazzled. Luckily it was the free one!

When I went to put something away in my wallet, my eye caught the little card that I always keep in there and I pulled it out. ***Count your blessings, not your worries.*** *"You will keep in perfect peace all who trust in you, whose thoughts are fixed on you!" Isaiah 26:3 (NLT)* That was just what I needed to read. I had spent so much of the day worrying, but worrying wouldn't change anything because God already had everything under control. If this surgery was meant to be, then God would get us to NYC, one way or another!

The wait went pretty quickly, thanks to some crossword puzzles I had packed. We also had some neat conversations with other people waiting which included a pilot who was also heading back to his family in NYC since the plane that he was going to pilot was canceled.

As the afternoon wore on trains were beginning to cancel and the farthest they were able to go north was to New York City. But we did board just a few minutes late. I really enjoyed the trip because I hadn't ridden a train in years. It was dark and snowing heavily so we really couldn't see anything out of the windows. Our car was so warm and the rocking of the car put me right to sleep.

The train arrived at the busy Penn Station in NYC at nearly 10 that night, and then we took the subway into Grand Central Station. We made it into NYC, yippee!

When we walked out into the streets we couldn't believe our eyes! The streets and sidewalks were covered with many inches of snow. It was windy and still snowing heavily, and it looked magical with the big snowflakes coming down, making me feel as if I was in a snow globe. People were lining the sidewalks taking pictures. We had to walk two blocks to our hotel, and was it ever a trek. It was slippery and we had to walk through some large drifts making it very difficult to stay in an upright position and not fall face first into the snow! There was no way to wheel our luggage so we had to carry it. We took plenty of breaks along the way and just couldn't stop laughing because nothing that day had gone the way we had originally planned, and we had experienced a lot in only a day's time! It was late but we felt wide awake by the time we reached our room so we unpacked and relaxed until after midnight.

That next morning we were up early because we had no idea what we'd be waking up to since it was still snowing when we went to bed. We read that the city had gotten two to three feet of snow depending on where you were located. My appointments were to start at nine that morning but since no taxis were able to drive, we knew that we'd have a lot of walking through the snow to do so we left fairly early. I was very glad that at the last minute I decided to pack my boots!

It was like a completely new world outside, and I am glad I got to experience this side of New York City also. Nobody was on the streets, and the city had an eeriness to it, because it was so quiet. Cars on the sides of the streets were piled high with snow and the city buses were even stuck in the middle of the streets. It was as if time stood still. The sidewalks were not cleared and there were big snow piles on almost all the street corners. Everyone was bundled up and walking and it was impossible to not have wet feet when reaching your destination!

We made it to the Hospital for Special Surgery with time to spare and went up to the third floor for my pre-surgical appointment. When I was there for my last surgery, the waiting room was so full that we had to wait in chairs outside of the waiting room. When we walked in this time, we were the only ones!

I checked in and saw that two other people had been there before my appointment that morning so we weren't the only crazy ones! It was nice because I didn't feel rushed and was able to take time and have conversations with all the people along the way.

I got registered and then went over some paperwork with the nurse, had an EKG done, and then the nurse attempted to take a blood sample from me. I say attempted because two nurses tried and then resorted to calling the phlebotomist, who finally found a vein that would give them just enough blood. I then went over to radiology to have a chest x-ray done, and didn't really have to wait there long either. Afterwards it was on to the 6th floor to meet with an internist, whom I'd also met with for my previous surgeries.

We had three hours until my next appointment with Dr. Boachie, but since not many people were at the waiting rooms in the hospital, mom suggested that we go over to his office and see if we could get an earlier appointment. We walked a block down to Dr. Boachie's office building and when the elevator opened at his floor, there were no patients in the waiting room, and I was taken right back.

Dr. Boachie and his fellow, Dr. Isaac, came in and talked with us about what he would be doing during my surgery. He was planning to remove part of the top portion of my right rod because it was quite prominently poking out of my middle back. We then asked about him possibly taking the anchor that went into my pelvis out also. Some days there was pain that shot down my upper leg and the pain management doctor felt that the anchor could possibly be the source of the pain. Dr. Boachie said that he could remove it but left the decision up to me. He said that there is a fifteen percent chance that the screw is causing the problem but since I've had many bone grafts taken out of my pelvis that could also be a cause of the pain I was experiencing. We'd never know unless he took it out, so it left me with something to think about.

It was a good appointment and we left at 12:30 which gave us the whole afternoon yet! Snow plows were then out trying to clear the main avenues but they had a long day ahead of them, that's for sure!

We ate at Blooms again, where I got some tortellini soup and them we rested a bit before venturing out again. We were on the subway going into Brooklyn when it stopped and everyone was told to disembark because there was a problem. We realized we were all feeling very exhausted because of the previous day's adventure so we decided to just take the train back into Manhattan. We went back to the hotel, watched TV, called my sisters, and then went to bed fairly early because the next morning would come early!

I was very surprised in the fact that I was hardly nervous at all, which was highly unusual for me. But the magnitude of this surgery was going to be so much less than my previous ones, which was what I kept telling myself! *"Peace I leave with you; my peace I give you. I do not give to you as the world gives. Do not let your hearts be troubled and do not be afraid." John 14:27 (NIV)*

December 28ᵗʰ arrived, and we were up bright and early because I had to be at the hospital at 6:00 am that morning. As I was doing my morning devotions before we left, I came across a verse that was not coincidental. *"Because Your love is better than life, my lips will glorify You. I will praise You as long as I live, and in Your name I will lift up my hands." Psalm 63:3-4 (NIV)* As much as I was not looking forward to another surgery and the discomfort it would bring, I knew that it was another part of God's plan for my life. I choose to praise God and look for the good in life no matter what the circumstance may be, because God's love for me is more powerful than anything else in this world.

We left the hotel at five since the roads still weren't all that great and we weren't sure how far we'd get in a taxi. Our taxi driver was pretty brave but almost got the taxi stuck when we were going down a side street, but we only had to walk one block to the hospital, since our driver didn't think that he'd be able to make it through.

We waited in the hospital lobby for a while and watched people come and go, and then headed up to the fourth floor surgery waiting room. The sun was just beginning to rise and looked very pretty over the East river.

I got registered and then was taken back to a pre-op room, which was next to the window! I changed into a gown and booties, got my vitals done, and then the parade of doctors began, starting with the nutritionist, Dr. Boachie's fellow and resident, and the surgical nurse, and the anesthesiology fellow. Then a patient care assistant came in and washed and sanitized my back. Then my anesthesiologist came in. He spent quite a bit of time talking and laughing with us and I immediately felt at ease. After he left, the nurse started the IV and Dr. Boachie came in and signed my incision sites. I decided to have him take out the anchor from my pelvis because there was a chance that removing that screw may solve some pain issues which I really wanted.

My surgery was scheduled to begin at eight but the minutes kept ticking by and nobody came to get me. Then at 8:30, my wonderful anesthesiologist came in and injected some medication into my IV, and I didn't think anything of it. He released the brakes on my bed, told me to give my parents a kiss, and then I was wheeled out. Well, he must have given me my heavy sedation medication because I don't even remember going through the "personnel only" doors. I remember being wheeled out of my pre-op room and that's it. I have never been out cold before going into the OR before, and was kind of disappointed because I liked meeting the people involved in my surgery beforehand.

The surgery didn't take long at all, only about an hour and a half. I do remember slightly waking up in the OR with the intubation tube in my mouth yet, because they were suctioning around it, and kept telling me to take deep breaths, because apparently I wasn't. I don't remember anything else though and was in a deep sleep for most of the day in the PACU.

The anesthesiologist was in one time when mom was visiting and was concerned as to why I wasn't waking up. I'd had a shorter surgery, and should have been awake more quickly, or so he thought, but for me that was not unusual. It always took me a long time to wake up from any of my surgeries because I was so sensitive to the medication.

My parents were allowed twenty minute visits along with the other patients' families, every few hours. At my parents' last visit at eight, the nurses weren't sure if I would be taken up to the floor or not because I was still not very alert, but at 10:30 that night I was wheeled up to the sixth floor.

My throat was really sore and whenever I took pills, I felt as if they got stuck in my throat and so I just pressed my PCA (pain) pump when I was awake, to get my pain medication. I don't remember much that night, other than my wonderful nurse coming in every few hours to help roll me over.

The next morning I was so tired and could hardly keep my eyes open. My physical therapist came in but I could only walk two steps because of the dizziness and nausea that overtook me. My parents then came in at ten-thirty, and stayed for an hour but I told them that I really needed to sleep for awhile and so they left me and went out for a walk.

I fell into a deep, blissful sleep, and then at 1:30 that afternoon, my physical therapist came in and found me unresponsive. She got my nurse, and then many others came in too. I could barely hear them and they sounded so far away if I did hear anything. Dr. Boachie's physician assistant was pinching my leg, and I heard her say that it should be very painful, but did I feel anything? Nope.

An anesthesiologist came in, who remembered me from when I had seizures during my last hospital stay. He massaged my chest with his knuckles, and then, with his hands, grabbed both sides of my jaw, pulling my head away from the bed. I could faintly hear what they were doing, but I couldn't feel anything. It was scary because I felt like I was trapped inside my body, because I could slightly hear but not respond. Then somebody brought some smelling salts for me to sniff, and were they powerful. They held them right under my nose, and when I breathed in, I coughed, but still couldn't wake up.

They put the oxygen on full blast, kept massaging my chest, and then brought the smelling salts out again. After a few minutes, I finally could wake up, although things were still a little fuzzy. I actually teared up, and they told me that they were taking me back down to the PACU to be monitored for a few hours.

They didn't think I had a seizure. I am just really sensitive to all the medication, and that caught up with me from the day before, because I hadn't pressed my PCA (pain) pump very often that morning. Mom and dad found out what had happened and went back down to the atrium to wait until they could see me again. I was put in a cubicle right next to the nurse's station, and hooked up to all the monitors.

By that time I was more awake, had a neighbor who talked loudly with any nurses who came close, and with all the noises in the PACU, it was very difficult to rest. I did get to watch TV without paying for it which was a bonus, although without my glasses on, it was very hard to see.

Two neurologists came in to check me over and made sure that nothing was wrong neurologically, and I checked out fairly normal. That evening, there was talk that I would have to stay overnight in the PACU, which I did not want, because it was so loud, and I was right next to the nurse's station. Luckily my wonderful anesthesiologist was making rounds later that night and cleared me to go back up to the sixth floor which made me very happy.

When I got up to my room, my favorite nurse that I had had for my last two surgeries, came in and talked with me for a little bit, which was nice. She wasn't my nurse that evening but it meant so much that she remembered me and came to say hello. Because my bed was right next to the window, I had a fantastic view and I loved watching the sunrise and sunset over the river.

Early Thursday morning, I also got a roommate who was a year older than I was. We never really talked because she was pretty sleepy from having surgery the night before, but she had a great family and we had some good conversations with them over the days I was there.

That morning I woke up feeling very nauseous and vomited twice - not a good way to start the day especially since Dr. Boachie's fellow had just come in to check on me. My blood sugar was low so the nurse gave me apple juice but every sip made me more nauseous. So they switched my medication and the new one worked much better.

Later on, my physical therapist came in and since I was much more alert, compared to the day before when she found me unresponsive, I was able to make a lap around the floor. My parents were given permission to take me for walks throughout the day also.

When we took walks, it was amazing how many people saw and remembered us from when I had surgery there the previous summer. Many people I didn't remember because I slept a lot, but it was so nice to talk with them and see some familiar faces.

For supper I got a real meal tray for the first time, since I had been on clear liquids earlier. That afternoon, all I could think about was eating a grilled cheese. I didn't get a grilled cheese, but real food did taste good again! Later on, Dr. Boachie came in, checked my incisions, and said that I could go home the next day, which was New Year's Eve, and made me excited.

After my parents left, I talked with my sister on the phone for awhile which was nice, since we were both a little lonely. That night it seemed so loud with many patients ringing their alarms, so sleep was difficult, and made me glad that it would be my last night sleeping there.

The next morning, which was Friday, I got washed up and dressed because I was going home, or I guess back to the hotel. Since it was a holiday things were a little slower than usual. By 11am when patients begin to be discharged I hadn't even seen Dr. Boachie's spine fellow. He finally came an hour later. Then all I needed to do was have my IV out and sign some papers. But the floor was busy with patients being discharged and the hours kept passing. We wondered if they had forgotten me.

At 4:00, my nurse finally came in, and getting me discharged only took five minutes. She said she'd find someone to take me down to the lobby in a wheelchair. Well, seeing how long we already had to wait to get discharged, we decided to sneak out since I could walk just fine and probably just looked like a visitor with my street clothes on. My roommate's family told us to go, and chuckled as we left! We made it but I was afraid we'd get in trouble.

Once out of the hospital we walked a block to find a taxi. It was New Year's Eve so finding a taxi was a challenge, especially with so many streets still closed. But we found one and made it back to the hotel an hour later. I leapt into the shower, but was careful to keep my incision dry and then we had dinner at Bloom's, and took a walk. There were horns honking in the streets and people were dressed up, which made me feel a little out of place in my sweat pants and tennis shoes, but I was at least comfortable and warm! Unfortunately, I couldn't stay up until midnight to watch the ball drop because my eyelids were so heavy. I guess I just expected the whole city to explode with sound at midnight, but it didn't, or if it did, I never woke up!

Since this surgery was much less invasive, I was able to get out and walk around, and wasn't too sore. We would often go out in the early afternoons, come back to the hotel to rest, and then in the evening, go out to dinner and take another walk.

On Sunday, I took my parents to the Redeemer Presbyterian Church, which was where I attended with my team when I was in the city six months earlier through Campus Crusade for Christ. After the service, we walked out to rain. Who would have thought that it would be raining just a few days after they had a blizzard?

We walked a few blocks up to our favorite Chinese restaurant and then went back to the hotel for an afternoon break. When we entered our room and turned the lights on, nothing happened. We all stood there, looking at each other. A woman who worked at the front desk had followed us up and told us there was no power in our room, along with all the rooms below us in that corner. She asked us if we would be willing to switch rooms, since the electrician had to come in from New Jersey and had many hours of work ahead of him. We really didn't have a choice since the room was very dark with no lights on, and the sun would be setting soon.

We initially were given a room two floors down and so dad and I took a few things down and dumped them on the bed. When we came back up, mom was chuckling and told us that we'd have to go back down to get the clothes because the woman found a better room for us that was on the same floor, just around the corner.

Oh, we had fun, and had quite the time laughing about yet another "bump" that was unexpected with this trip. When everything was finally sorted and put away I was exhausted, and turned the TV on, although most of it was watched with my eyes closed.

The next day was not a good day for me. I guess all the running around had caught up with me because I was really hurting. Even so, I had wanted to see the Museum of Natural History so we went. We had to take breaks whenever we found a bench and we had to leave after an hour or so because I was so worn out and in pain.

On our way back to the hotel we found a Crumb's Bakeshop and had to stop. They are known for their cupcakes in every flavor imaginable. The cupcakes were huge, with a mound of delicious, creamy frosting on top, and some of them even have a creamy filling in the center! We stood admiring all of the different cupcakes for quite a while because it was difficult to choose. We finally agreed on two cupcakes to split among the three of us, and they were absolutely fabulous! After an afternoon of resting and relaxing, I was ready to go out for our nightly stroll. It was our last night in the city.

I had mixed emotions that last night as I was lying in bed, not sleeping. There is just something about being in NYC that just seems to bring out my self confidence. I suppose it is because I have to know how to get different places by public transportation, and not look lost, like a tourist! I love living in Ohio, but there is just something about the city that draws me, and a longing deep inside of me to someday live in NYC after I finish my college degree, which seems to be a never ending process!

The next day, January 5, the weather was great - a perfect day for flying. So there was no chance of delays, right? Just as we were ready to board it was announced that our plane was having mechanical problems but would be ready shortly. Our one hour connection in Philadelphia was becoming shorter and shorter.

An hour later it was announced that we were being transferred to another plane at the other end of the terminal. We finally took off at the same time we were supposed to be landing in Philadelphia. We landed there with only ten minutes to connect with our flight to Detroit. We jumped on the shuttle bus, then ran to our gate. So much for enjoying our layover. What a laugh we had because that is just how the whole trip had gone for us! We were the last three people to board and my seat was in the very last row. But we made it!

It was good to sleep in my own bed that night, and not have to worry about bedbugs anymore, unless we brought some home. New York City had had problems with bed bugs spreading in years past, and was beginning to have an infestation throughout the city again, which always made me paranoid the first night that we stayed in a hotel there. I always felt as if something was crawling on my legs, but it was just my imagination!

* * *

Less than two weeks after having surgery was my first day back at college, which was rather tiring, and didn't help that the first day of classes we had a massive snowstorm. This made concentrating in my classes rather difficult when I could see the snow piling up on the cars outside, and wondering how the drive home was going to be. I noticed I was able to sit back against my chair in class without pain and I had to remind myself to sit back because I was so used to leaning forward to prevent the pain.

Then I heard the voice of the Lord saying, "Whom shall I send? And who will go for us?" And I said, "Here am I. Send me!" Isaiah 6:8 (NIV) Towards the end of January, I finally found out that I was accepted into the Campus Crusade for Christ STINT overseas program. I wouldn't know my official campus location until the intern kickoff weekend which would be held in the spring. I was so excited!

A month later I got a long awaited letter in the mail. "Dear Libbey, It is my pleasure to inform you that the Surgical Technologies Admissions Committee has recommended your acceptance into the class beginning the Fall 2012 Semester. Congratulations!" Wow, I had been waiting to see those words for a very long time! The timing could not be more perfect. I would be coming home after being overseas for a year, and three weeks later would begin the surgical tech program at college. I am continuing to be in awe of the wondrous love and perfect timing our Heavenly Father has for us.

As I look ahead in my future I wonder many things. Will I begin leaning again? Will I need more spine surgeries? Will I live with constant pain the rest of my life? Will my GI issues resolve or will more intervention be necessary? I don't know what my future will hold, but none of us do. There's no need to dwell on the future, but instead live one day at a time, for our days are numbered.

"..this happened so that the work of God might be displayed in his life." John 9:3b (NIV) I don't believe that I would be the woman I am today without having gone through the trials of these past six years. I've had to sacrifice and give up many opportunities, but so many doors have been opened for me as well.

Everlasting, Your light will shine when all else fades. Never ending, Your glory goes beyond all fame. My heart and my soul, I give you control. Consume me from the inside out Lord. Let justice and praise, become my embrace to love You from the inside out. This song "From The Inside Out" by Hillsong United could not be more true. This is the cry of my heart, my deepest longing, that I would love the Lord with all of my heart, from the inside out, and that my actions and words would also come to show that my love for Him is pure.

When the storms of life try to overtake me, His hope always shines in the distance no matter how near or far away it seems. His eternal hope is the one thing we can hold on to forever.

A Father's Perspective

Looking back I see all the lives being touched by Libbey. Doctors and nurses that cared for Libbey, friends and family that helped us in so many ways, and people helping financially through benefits that were done for Libbey. Just one blessing after another happened throughout the years. Where does our strength come from? Our strength comes from the Lord! I have tried to learn to trust in the Lord for all things. It's really hard sometimes for me but I see where He has worked in really neat ways through Libbey's journey. She has been a real inspiration to me and I know to many other people also.

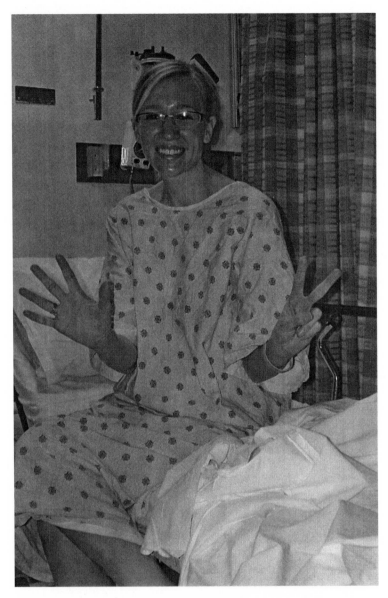

On December 28, 2010, I had my seventh surgery in NYC. It was by far the least complex surgery I had with my rods trimmed down and my pelvic anchor removed. I am pictured above holding seven figures up for my seventh surgery.

I had physical therapy two times each day after my seventh surgery.

Epilogue

"Give thanks to the Lord, call on His name; make known among the nations what He has done. Sing to Him, sing praise to Him; tell of His wonderful acts." Psalm 105:1-2 (NIV)

Many people have told me that I should write a book, and at first I wasn't quite sure about it, because I am a very private person. The more I thought about it, the more I felt as if I should write this book. There are not many books written about people sharing their journey with scoliosis, which I found frustrating when I was first diagnosed in 2005. Although many who have scoliosis will not have quite the same journey, just knowing there is someone else out there who felt as you do is always uplifting.

All along, since my very first appointment, I kept a journal of what happened - each test and appointment - and that helped me in writing the book. My journey is not over and will probably be something that I will be dealing with most of my life. I have a deep desire to do medical mission work in Africa someday. In the nearer future, I hope to get my surgical tech certificate, and would love to get a job in Manhattan, NYC, maybe even at the Hospital for Special Surgery! In the back of my mind, I still have thoughts of returning to school to study nursing after I receive my surgical tech certificate and have experience working in that field. Only God knows what my future holds, and I am excited to see what He has in store for me!

Along my journey, many have asked how I can keep smiling and stay positive about life when dealing with a spinal deformity. This deformity has not only been painful, but has also made me very self conscious since I was in a brace for many of my teenage years. My family has been, and continues to be, very supportive and has offered me much encouragement throughout this journey. I have also been helped by many great medical personnel, including nurses and skilled surgeons like Dr. Munk and Dr. Boachie.

I don't know how I would have made it through the past few years without my faith. There were times when I was just ready to stop searching and getting opinions from new doctors, but I knew that since I was still alive and breathing that God had a plan for my life. He was not finished with me yet on this earth, although there were times when I wished He was because the pain was almost too much to handle. There are so many people in this world who are silently suffering everyday because they have no access to adequate medical care, and I have been thankful that I did, even if I was tired of going from doctor to doctor. At times it is easy to feel as if you are at your limit and ready to give up, but looking back on past experiences you can look at how God has sustained you. With God, we can truly be strong enough to endure the trials of life.

This has been quite a journey, but an amazing one as well. It's a journey I would have never chosen to take had I been asked. Through this experience, I have met so many incredible people, people whose paths I never would have crossed had I not had countless tests, procedures, and surgeries performed. These people have touched my life in many ways that they will never know, and I hope that in some small way, I touched theirs as well.

**Jesus, sometimes it is hard to understand things in life. We are constantly experiencing both mountains and valleys. Although reaching the mountain tops of life can be exhilarating, it is in the valleys that builds us into the people we are today, and has drawn me closer to You. If we believe in You, everything, both positive and negative, will be worth it in the end because we have You, and eternal life. Nothing can beat that! I love You! **

Acknowledgments

Where to begin the list of people to thank? There have been so many who have blessed my life in so many different ways and have supported me physically, emotionally, financially, and spiritually and I thank them all. When I was first diagnosed with scoliosis, I couldn't have imagined the journey that it would take me on over the next few years, but there have been so many people who have encouraged and supported me along the way.

First, I need to thank my Heavenly Father because He has given me the daily strength and hope to keep going and continues to give my life meaning. Sweet Jesus, through my many trials you have shown me that nothing is too big to come between my relationship with You.

Dr. Munk, you have meant so much more to me than you probably know. Over the past few years, you have seen me at both the best and worst times of my life. You have never given up on trying to find the source of my rapid spinal decompensation, and have presented my case to in front of so many other surgeons throughout the world at conferences, which is so greatly appreciated.

Helen (Dr. Munk's nurse), you have waved your magic wand many times and have coordinated so many appointments for me over the years. We never could have scheduled all of them without you! Being wheeled back into surgery is always a nerve wracking experience but you were there right beside me and held my hand until I was completely sedated those first four surgeries, which was so comforting.

Dr. Boachie, when I was feeling as if I was going to be in a back brace the rest of my life, you gave me a hope that I never expected to hear. You took the risk of correcting my spine even more than it already was and with the help of physical therapy I am standing straight again! I really admire your devotion to give back to the people of Africa, which is one of my heart's desires too.

To my grandparents, mom, dad, Rebekah, Katie, Derek, and Annie, you guys have supported me throughout this journey. You were my biggest cheering section when I felt down and in need of encouragement. You have taken off work to come be with me before surgery even though the majority of my surgeries required you to get up extremely early. That meant the world to me! When I had trouble eating, if I ever expressed a desire for a certain something, their one of you would be baking/cooking it for me! Words alone cannot express my deep love and appreciation towards all of you!

To my many prayer warriors, financial supporters, and people who sent cards over the years I am so thankful for your support. I truly believe in the power of prayer, and each time I went into surgery, I knew that so many were lifting my doctors, family, and me up in prayer. I always felt a great burden when I would see the many medical bills come in the mail, but through the financial support of many, this weight had been lifted off of my shoulders. Over the past few years I have received hundreds of cards, which always made a big impact on my life. Each card brought its own way of touching my life whether by making me laugh, or providing comfort and encouragement. I thank you from the bottom of my heart!

I wish I could sit down and thank everyone I know that was involved in my care, but the list would be endless! A special thanks to all of my nurses, technicians, and doctors who helped get me to where I am today! I am so grateful and hope to one day be working beside you in the health care field! Thank you so very much.

"Keep Believing In Yourself"

There may be days
when you get up in the morning
and things aren't the way
you had hoped they would be
That's when you have to
tell yourself that things will get better.

There are times when people
disappoint you and let you down,
but those are the times
when you must remind yourself
to trust your own judgments and opinions,
and to keep your life focused on believing in yourself
and all that you are capable of.

There will be challenges to face
and changes to make in your life,
and it is up to you to accept them.
Constantly keep yourself headed
in the right directions for you.
It may not be easy at times,
but in those times of struggle
you will find a stronger sense of who you are,
and you will also see yourself
developing into the person
you have always wanted to be.

Life is a journey through time,
filled with many choices;
each of us will experience life
in our own special way.

So when the days come that are filled
with frustration and unexpected responsibilities,
remember to believe in yourself
and all you want your life to be,
because the challenges and changes
will only help you to find the dreams
that you know are meant to come true for you.

-Author Unknown-

Permissions

Chapter 6
"In Christ Alone," written by Keith Getty/Stuart Townend Copyright 2002 Thankyou Music (PRS) (adm. worldwide at EMICMGPublishing.com excluding Europe which is adm. by Kingswaysongs) All rights reserved. Used by permission.

Chapter 22
"You Are Everything," written by Sam Mizell/Matthew West Copyright 2008 Simple Tense Songs & Wyzell Music (ASCAP) admin. by Simpleville Music, Inc. /Word Music & Songs For Lulu (ASCAP)

Chapter 30
"Healing Hand Of God," written by Jeremy Camp Copyright 2008 Stolen Pride Music (ASCAP) Thirsty Moon River Publ. Inc. (ASCAP) (adm. at EMICMGPublishing.com) All rights reserved. Used by permission.

Chapter 35
"From The Inside Out," written by Joel Houston Copyright 2005 Hillsong Publishing (APRA) All rights reserved. Used by permission.

CPSIA information can be obtained at www.ICGtesting.com
Printed in the USA
268330BV00002B/5/P